# THE POLITICAL ECONOMY OF AID AND ACCOUNTABILITY

*To my mother and the memory of my father*

# The Political Economy
# of Aid and Accountability
## The Rise and Fall of Budget Support in Tanzania

HELEN TILLEY
*Overseas Development Institute, UK*

Routledge
Taylor & Francis Group

LONDON AND NEW YORK

First published 2014 by Ashgate Publishing

Published 2016 by Routledge
2 Park Square, Milton Park, Abingdon, Oxfordshire OX14 4RN
711 Third Avenue, New York, NY 10017, USA

First issued in paperback 2016

*Routledge is an imprint of the Taylor & Francis Group, an informa business*

**British Library Cataloguing in Publication Data**
A catalogue record for this book is available from the British Library

**The Library of Congress has cataloged the printed edition as follows:**
Tilley, Helen
  The political economy of aid and accountability : the rise and fall of budget support in Tanzania / by Helen Tilley.
     pages cm
  Includes bibliographical references and index.
  ISBN 978-1-4094-6442-6 (hardback : alk. paper)
1.  Finance, Public—Tanzania—Accounting.
2. Responsibility—Tanzania. 3. Economic assistance—Tanzania. I. Title.
  HJ9929.T34 T55
  338.9109678—dc23

                                                                2013043672


ISBN 13: 978-1-138-24718-5 (pbk)
ISBN 13: 978-1-4094-6442-6 (hbk)

# Contents

# List of Figures and Tables

**Figures**

**Tables**

# Acknowledgements

This research was possible because of the help and guidance received from many colleagues, friends and organisations.

I would like to thank my friends in Tanzania who generously gave their time and openly shared their views and understanding. Colleagues in Dar es Salaam at the Ministry of Finance, the European Commission and the Department for International Development helped me to develop my thoughts. Colleagues at ODI provided a constant flow of ideas that have made it difficult to stop writing. I would like to express my gratitude to Professor Jane Harrigan at the School of Oriental and African Studies for her encouragement, guidance and mentoring. I have been fortunate to have had many discussions with development professionals over the years and although they may not agree with all of my analyses, if this book is of interest to them then my research will have served a useful purpose.

Friends and family have, throughout the different stages of my research, provided much needed support. My largest debt is to my parents who have been unconditionally tolerant and encouraging. The sustenance of friends along the way has been cherished, especially Andy, Hazel, Evelyn, Jasma, Nicola and Heather. I would particularly like to thank Mike for his support. There are many others who I would also like to thank, some of whom may not realise the extent to which they have assisted me.

This research was enabled by fieldwork grants from the University of London Central Research Fund, the British Institute in East Africa, and the School of Oriental and African Studies. The Commission for Science and Technology, COSTECH, granted me permission to conduct research in Tanzania and I would like to thank them and the local government authorities of Ilala, Dar es Salaam and Dodoma for allowing me to conduct my research.

I am indebted to the many authors upon whose work I have drawn and from whom I have learnt so much, from the work of early philosophers to contemporary economists and political scientists. The clarity of their writings and the creativity of their thought made this research a pleasure to undertake.

I would like to acknowledge the help I received from Rob Sorsby at Ashgate in addressing all of the expected-unexpected events; Heather Budge-Reid for early structural inspiration; and Roo Griffiths for early editorial input. I am grateful to Ruth Larbey and Ryan Flynn for their editorial support and for being exceptional in their thoroughness and insightful in their comments. All errors and omissions remain mine.

# Chapter 1
# Introducing Accountability: The Old and the New

## 1.1 Introduction

Governance, political-economy and economics literature have characterised accountability in many ways, with its usage evolving over time. In development discourse, the term became popularised in the late 1990s through the 'good governance' agenda (Cornwall 2007: 479). Accountability is often an implicit ideal in development and foreign aid, and has been most often understood in terms of particular, recognised relationship structures that can be expected to operate in predefined ways. These traditional conceptualisations of accountability can be described as *procedural*. While it is commonly recognised that stronger accountability relationships between all those involved in the service-delivery chain are important for development and improved quality of life (World Bank 2003), it is not just *stronger relationships* but rather a *different understanding* of accountability that is necessary. This book makes a radical departure from the traditional way of looking at accountability and applies a new understanding to the aid environment in Tanzania. The form of accountability presented here calls for an understanding of the wider socio-political context, within which aid is firmly situated. The constraints faced by aid agencies have, on the whole, prevented them from adjusting their approach to delivering aid.

The adherence of aid agencies to the good governance framework has the advantage of presenting a standard framework that overcomes the need for extensive country-specific knowledge, which is difficult to deliver under increasingly tight budget constraints (Booth 2012). The term 'accountability' and the frameworks of 'procedural accountability' are reassuring: they imply measurability. Financial and governance indicators or national audits, for example, indicate that the problem is identifiable and understood. Perhaps even more reassuring is the set of predictable solutions that should be applied: tougher regulation that results in better oversight and the application of penalties for non-conformity (Weisband and Ebrahim 2007). The implicit ideal of global accountability in development and foreign aid involves placing a negative value judgement on practices that do not conform to such measurable standards.

The understanding of accountability that is needed to resolve this problem is less contractual in nature and more accurately reflects the complexities of socioeconomic contexts. *Relational* accountability deals with issues of power and information asymmetries – and the realities of social and political structures – more effectively than traditional conceptions of accountability. It is a complementary concept, however: when considered alongside procedural accountability, it allows for a fuller understanding of how accountability operates in practice. The reference framework changes from presenting a set of one-sided problems and solutions (such as how one group can enforce other groups to act in certain ways), towards understanding the complexity of real relationships (and how all parties face constraints), by framing problems and finding solutions by individuals acting 'collectively in their own best interests' (Booth 2012: 11).

An enhanced understanding of accountability needs to distinguish, and recognise the interaction between traditional and rationalist accountability (procedural accountability) and a broader and more culturally relevant understanding of accountability (relational accountability). This book highlights how these different types of accountability interact and support one another. It examines how accountability operates in practice and how this is related to the decline of general budget support in the specific case of Tanzania.

## 1.2 The Procedural Approach to Accountability

Accountability may be either 'hard' or 'soft'. In its hard form, it fills the role of enforcing appropriate behaviour, with the threat of sanction (Fox 2007, Schedler 1999). In contrast, under soft accountability, one party is merely answerable for their actions to another party, without enforcement. Procedural, or traditional, accountability is often understood through the horizontal–vertical (H–V) accountability framework (presented in more detail below). By examining the economic concepts of 1) methodological individualism and 2) public-choice theory, which assumes individuals make rational choices based on the maximisation of their utility, we can better understand the weaknesses of the procedural accountability approach.

We can break the H–V framework down into its two components, the horizontal and the vertical. Horizontal accountability is the capacity of agencies of restraint (such as law courts, ombudspersons, audit offices, electoral tribunals, central banks, the media, trade unions and lawyers guilds) to ensure other branches of government are answerable for their actions. Thus, horizontal accountability is effected through the restraints that institutions of *equal status* impose on each other. It highlights the distinction between the powerful agencies of the state, and the less powerful agencies of society and individual actors, and requires a clear division of powers between state agencies, in the form of jurisdictions that are respected and upheld.

Vertical accountability refers to the state–citizen relationship, or the relationship between *unequals,* and the holding to account of public officials through actions of democracy, such as elections, civil society and the media: in other words, 'making elected officials answerable to the ballot box' (O'Donnell 1994: 61). Our discussion of vertical accountability focuses on democratic accountability,

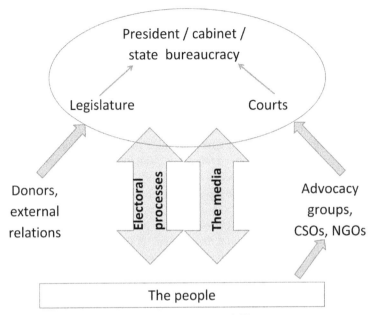

**Figure 1.1    Horizontal and vertical accountability**
*Source:* Adapted from Rakner (2005) ODI workshop on aid, budgets and accountability.

taxation and international accountability, where principals (the less powerful) demand accountability from agents (the more powerful). Vertical accountability can be demanded, such as the media requesting an explanation for an adverse audit report finding, inter-electoral participation in politics, electoral turnout, or by citizens using their voice to demand answerability. It can also relate to supply: for example, through the government voluntarily creating forums in which citizens can freely ask questions, the construction of state institutions of accountability, or the promotion of democratic interactions. Democracy is the main transmission mechanism through which H–V accountability can be considered to work. The literature has widely criticised this concept of democratic accountability and, by extension, vertical accountability, for not capturing the complexities of reality.

Although the basic procedural accountability model is useful, simplicity limits its utility. To increase its relevance for development discourse, we extend it by introducing nuances. While the H–V framework can be extended to incorporate these complexities, the assumption remains that the relationship is static and it cannot easily address dynamic adjustments in accountabilities or even overlapping accountabilities.

*The Weaknesses of Procedural Accountability*

A number of writers highlight the limitations involved in restricting understanding to the procedural form of accountability (Bovens 1998, Ebrahim 2009,

Eyben 2007, Gulrajani 2010). In this book, we analyse the weaknesses of procedural accountability by critiquing the methodological framework and deconstructing the assumptions embodied in the term 'accountability' and its applications. These underlying assumptions and concepts include rationality; motivation; individuals or actors; and power and society.

The overly simplistic H–V framework, while it can be adjusted for complexities, struggles with the possibility of dynamic recursive accountability and overlapping accountabilities (in horizontal accountability), and the political reality in developing countries of clientelism and patrimonial politics (in vertical accountability). The H–V model rests on a principal–agent framework where relationships are fixed and power is unequal, so that less powerful principals demand accountability from more powerful agents.

The nature of politics, however, is that 'ties of solidarity' result in leaders never being separated from their supporters and actions being based on a continual 'calculus of patrimonial reciprocity' (Chabal and Daloz 1999: 39). Many developing countries have legislatures that *appear* to be representative, but underneath, powerful interest groups operate, serving well-established political settlements and clientelistic interests. To move beyond the scope of procedural accountability, pertinent issues include the balance between powerful groups with allegiances to the state; the extent of bias and capture; and the role such issues play in the accountability context in today's developing countries.

Collective action can be considered a more fitting framework of analysis as it better reflects the challenges that all parties face in solving problems (Booth 2012). The collective-action problem relates to the under-provision of public goods (and services), often because of their non-excludable characteristic, and because the beneficiary group is large. This results in the cost being incurred by those who provide the good, and others – who do not contribute towards the cost of provision – free-riding on their initial investment (Olson 1965, Ostrom 1990). This problem can be seen as underpinning the entire discussion around accountability because, were it not for inability to provide social goods, or for information asymmetry, there would not be a need for formal accountability mechanisms.

Development problems can be challenging to solve, as collective identities in modern sub-Saharan Africa are unlikely to be organised in the straightforward way that one might expect. Alongside the reluctance to incur first-mover costs or to have others free-riding on their investment, individuals exit from situations of dissonance. Analysis of group behaviour in developing countries points to more complex, multifaceted problems that are better explained by collective action rather than the principal–agent perspective (Booth 2012). In addition, short-term interests may differ from long-term interests, introducing time inconsistency.

Issues missing from the H–V framework, and from procedural accountability, include the complexity of the network of accountability and the personal nature of the accountability within patronage relationships. The reality is a fragmentation of identities that include the religious, ethnic, geographical, economic, occupational and aspirational (Kelsall 2004). A circle of trust, or a large and dynamic support web, is the most likely result (Chabal and Daloz 1999, Kelsall 2004), rather than the homogeneous economic actor with a predetermined utility function that procedural accountability implies.

The restrictive assumptions of the procedural notion of accountability thus result in limited explanatory power. A weakness, therefore, in the traditional procedural understanding of accountability is the lack of a comprehensive analysis of the highly context-specific and complex cultural factors that underlie the relationships around which accountability is formed. These factors are based on interpersonal relationships between actors, capturing the interplay between actors and social institutions. This understanding of accountability is complex, highly personalised, underpinned by implicit and informal rules, and is a function of the specific political and social relations.

Underpinning the criticisms of procedural accountability are assumptions and theoretical roots located at different levels of analysis: the individual, the institutional and the structural. Linking these different levels we can ask several questions. If there are influences beyond utility maximisation on individual behaviour, where do these come from? Furthermore, who are the individuals or agents who are motivated, and what is their influence on units of economic organisation? What is the interaction between these different factors: between the individual agent and the economic unit, organisation or institution, and, temporally, between the behavioural outcome and the influence on future behaviour? We explore these issues through an application of Williamson's (2000) levels of social analysis (Figure 1.2, below). Lastly, if there is a need for a different analytical framework that brings in higher-level factors such as social norms and historical legacies, what does this mean for the methodological approach?

### 1.3 Understanding Accountability and Foreign Aid through a Political-Economy Lens

The procedural concept of accountability overlooks complexity, informality and clientelism because it is generally missing a political, economic and sociological understanding. Political economy broadly refers to the interaction between politics and economics, with a specific consideration of incentives and the competition around resources based on the enactment of power, with the social and historical context seen as central to the analysis. Failure to apply a political-economy approach to accountability's challenges in aid has resulted in continued inappropriate and misaligned expectations for donors, and subsequent conflict between donors and recipient governments. As this book discusses, the concept of relational accountability is a political-economy approach.

Despite the limitations of the procedural model, it has come to dominate international relations as part of the public-management ethos. Its implicit rationalist economic epistemology is based on certain international best practices and standards and assumes motivations of actors and agencies, who are predicted to maximise their own individual interests in certain ways (Gulrajani 2010).

To fully understand how relational accountability operates, it is essential to appreciate the role of history in constructing social relations over time. Complexity ensues: each individual has a web of different relations, each embodying a set of incentives, and thus his or her approach to accountability.

Incentives can also be understood as motivations – 'the organisation of an actor's wants' – which involves conscious and unconscious emotions and cognition (Giddens 1979: 58). In the aid context, examples of donor incentives to disburse aid include: the avoidance of economic chaos risked by non-receipt of aid inflows and negative impacts on the poor; political clientelism; the risk of not servicing debt; the career interests of aid agency personnel; and the maintenance of the reputation of the agency (Kanbur 2000). Recipient government incentives can be separated into the international and the national: internationally, governments want to keep donors on board to ensure aid is received; nationally, they want to obtain voter support.

The interaction of incentives determines behavioural outcomes. Of course, the complexity of different incentives and how they interact with the context result in the outcomes being very changeable; they may even appear to be contradictory. Incentives are embedded within the personal relations between agents, which, in turn, respond to social norms through their interaction with the social structure.

Incentives may be financial, power and status related, or even emotional, and may be based on future expectations rather than simply immediate results. As a result, the political-economy approach takes a longer-term perspective and is characterised by rules that are informal and complex, emerge unexpectedly and are likely to have evolved over a longer period of time. This sits in the higher levels of the hierarchy of social analysis, presented below, which we use to frame the two concepts of accountability.

*A Hierarchy of Social Analysis*

Williamson (2000) presents a tiered framework for social analysis that distinguishes between micro theories (the neoclassical methodological individualist approach at the bottom) and macro theories (institutional and structural approaches at the top) (Figure 1.2). This is a useful framework for our analysis, as it highlights the epistemologically different roots of the two types of accountability.

The top level (Level 1) is the focus of the work of economic historians and sociologists and is the location of norms and traditional and embedded elements, such as cognitive, cultural, structural and political factors. Much social analysis takes these factors as exogenous, as they more or less remain constant, only changing across centuries or millennia. This captures the relational characteristics of longer-term change, the importance of the wider social system and its nuances, and the informal role of norms of behaviour.

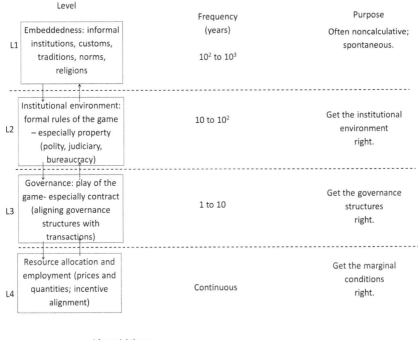

Figure 1.2    A hierarchy of analysis

*Source:* Williamson (2000)

*Note:* * The frequency at which change can occur within each level, ranging from 1,000 years (Level 1) to continual change (Level 4)

The lower levels are where procedural accountability can be found, as rules become formalised within a contractual basis. Level 2 concerns the institutional environment, where formal rules and regulations are located, and the legislative structure determines the structure and operation of state agencies, including the executive, the parliament and the legislature. Level 3 is the location of the operational rules of governance structures. It focuses on the impact of governance structures on incentives and, given the emphasis on the contract, changes take place alongside contract renewals at a frequency of between a year and a decade. Finally in the procedural realm, in Level 4 the firm and the consumer are the units of analysis within which continual adjustments to price and quantity take place.

The higher levels of the analysis impose restrictions on the lower levels such that changes in Levels 3 and 4 can only occur within the boundaries dictated by Level 1, firstly, and subsequently Level 2. In the short term, change is restricted to micro elements such as price and quantity; in the medium-term, change at the level of governance institutions within Level 3 can occur, for instance, as contracts are renewed. However, only the longer term permits institutional adjustments to state institutions. All of these changes are framed within the cognitive, cultural and normative rules of society captured in Level 1. The restrictions that the higher levels impose on the lower levels are such that the particular cultural setting restricts the range of governance institutions that can be accepted within a particular society and in turn dictates those that function successfully. Where a change is imposed that does not accord with the higher-level structures, discord results in either 1) the alien element being rejected, after a period of conflict and tension, or 2) an adjustment to the higher structures to incorporate the new element. This accords with the etymology of hierarchy noted by Simon whereby, within a formal system, each tier is a subordinate subsystem situated within and responsive to the authority of a higher tier (Simon 1962).

We next look at the pitfalls of not incorporating political economy into understandings of accountability, as we present a relational, as opposed to a purely procedural, approach.

## 1.4  Developing a New Approach: Relational Accountability

The discussion above illustrates the need for an additional form of accountability, one that considers complex, highly personalised and often contradictory political and social relations, based on implicit, informal and accidental rules.

Relational accountability is developed from a multidisciplinary understanding of culture; the interface between agency and structure; critiques of rationality; the positioning of the state in society; and the role of elites and power. It is defined as the accountability that is embodied within the personal relations between actors, which, in turn, respond to social norms through their interaction with the social structure. Elites are at the core of the analysis, given the pivotal role they play in influencing policies and decisions, linking the state and society. This core is fluid and its reach of accountability stretches out in a web-like structure capturing actors as they function within a multitude of different social roles within elite networks. Relational accountability depends on the process of power at play in all relations and is subtly demonstrated through language. It allows for an analysis of the role of obligations and patronage in a reciprocal relationship that is influenced by social norms, culture and power.

Relational accountability views the nature of power differently from procedural accountability.[1] Through the procedural accountability lens, power is a contractual resource that is limited. Through the relational accountability lens, power is ubiquitous, underpinning all interactions, and implicitly shapes perceptions and views. Furthermore, it is represented ideologically through language, and

---

1    This is summarised here and discussed in detail in Chapter 3.

**Table 1.1    Procedural accountability and relational accountability compared**

| Parameter | Procedural accountability | Relational accountability |
|---|---|---|
| Context | Specific and close | Wider social system<br>Political and social relations |
| Focus | Mechanisms for regulating behaviour | Clientelistic relations |
| Rules | Contractual and formal<br>Simplified | Informal<br>Complex<br>Implicit and accidental |
| Measured | By financial and governance indicators | Not measured |
| Power | Contractual, e.g. performance-assessment framework<br>A resource<br>Limited | An implicit process underpinning all interactions<br>Unlimited and ubiquitous<br>A capacity that may not be enacted |
| Constraints and problem solving | Principal–agent approach dominant | Collective-action approach dominant, within which principal–agent relationships may operate |

*Source*: Author's concepts of procedural and relational accountability defined using parameters developed from Eyben (2007).

subtly underpins styles of communication. Procedural accountability assumes a principal–agent framework where less powerful principals demand accountability from more powerful agents. However, in a more complex reality, where there are multiple actors, each with their own problems to solve, collective action better reflects the array of challenges of all parties. Power is enacted through clientelistic networks: explicitly, when the more powerful clients impose constraints on the state and the payoffs reflect their relative power (Khan 2004a); and covertly through the shaping of perceptions. This arises as the boundaries between the public and the private are blurred, and because there is an informalisation of power (Bratton and Van de Walle 1997, Chabal and Daloz 1999, Jackson and Rosberg 1982, Médard 1982). Table 1.1 compares the two different types of accountability.

Political economy is at the core of the concept of relational accountability, and it is important to understand why. Looking at the role of history in constructing social relations over time brings to the fore the complexity of relational accountability, as each individual has a web of different relations, each embodying a set of incentives. The interaction of these determines behavioural outcomes. The complexity of the different incentives and how they may interact with the context mean the outcomes are highly changeable and may appear contradictory. The incentives are embedded within the personal relations between agents, which, in

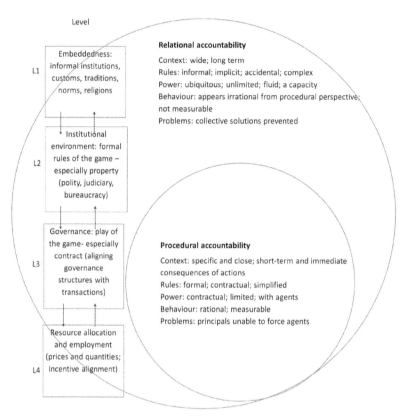

**Figure 1.3      Procedural and relational accountability within
                  Williamson's framework**

*Source:* Author's adaptation of Williamson (2000)

turn, respond to social norms through their interaction with the social structure. The traditional or procedural concept of accountability overlooks these elements, and therefore falls short of a political-economy understanding.

Placing the two different concepts of accountability in Williamson's hierarchy, procedural accountability resides within Levels 2, 3 and 4, and exists within the broader concept of relational accountability, which is located at Level 1, and has a deeper and more durable structure. Relational accountability therefore provides the framework within which procedural accountability can function. If an occurrence arises through procedural accountability that does not fit within the boundaries of the higher-level relational accountability, discord will result. This can lead to conflict in the form of game playing, and tension in the need for adjustment could result in either rejection of the procedural accountability demand or a shift in the relational accountability part of the framework.

Figure 1.3 places the two forms of accountability within Williamson's framework and summarises the assumptions. Relational accountability, the broader and more culturally relevant understanding of accountability, sits at the highest tier, and therefore presents the boundaries for the operation of procedural accountability, which sits below. The context of procedural accountability is immediate and specific, whereas that of relational accountability relates to the wider social system. Procedural accountability has a short-term timeframe and focuses on the immediate consequences of actions, whereas relational accountability takes a longer-term perspective, such that immediate repayment for social favours is not a necessity. The rules underpinning procedural accountability are formalised and simplified in contracts; relational accountability is characterised by rules that can be informal, highly complex, and accidental, and may have evolved over a period of time.

Relational accountability is subject to some of the critiques that have been levied at procedural accountability. Procedural accountability is based on methodological individualism, but relational accountability is also an actor-centric approach, although this is modified as the actor is placed firmly within structures and there is continual feedback and a multitude of crossovers within and between the different social structures and the individual. In combining procedural accountability and relational accountability, we aim to present a model that embodies the formal and contractual where it is present, but also allows for complexity and acknowledges the challenges of collective action. In this exploration we aim to provide specific examples that illustrate how procedural accountability and relational accountability are interrelated and how they coexist.

The' model of accountability constructed in this book focuses on the central government public sector and how this interacts with the international development community through the delivery of budget support. In the international aid environment, there is a meeting of actors from different cultures, yet these operate within a non-Western societal context. In analysing this, Chapters 5 and 6 apply the model to the context in Tanzania.

## 1.5 Bringing in Relational Accountability: Moving to an Application in Tanzania

To find a model of accountability that can be applied in Tanzania, we must draw out the interaction and mutual dependency of the two types of accountability. Procedural accountability is imposed as a tool through which donors understand the development context, embodied in processes. However, its operation sits within the relational accountability context, where the real challenge is solving collective action problems in a complex environment. Therefore, we must adopt both lenses to enable a fuller understanding and recognise that both types of accountability are ideal types that are unlikely to exist in their pure form.

As we have seen, procedural accountability is a 'Western' concept and is based implicitly on an epistemology whereby actors, either principals or agents, are rational utility maximisers, transactions are impersonal, rules are formal and contractual in nature, and the pursuit of self-interest is assumed to lead to moral hazard in the absence of full information. The accountability contract arises when a principal exercises authority over an agent's actions, the authority being embodied in a judgement of whether responsibilities have been met and assessed against objective and externally specified standards (Grant and Keohane 2005). As these assumptions are overly simple, and overlook instances when collection action is a more appropriate framework, they have only limited application in reality.

## 1.6  Book Structure

The book commences with Chapter 2, which explores procedural accountability in depth, using the H–V framework. This forms the basis from which we can deconstruct its assumptions, move towards a new understanding of accountability, and then see how the two types operate together. The H–V accountability framework discussed in Chapter 2 is based on a power relationship, as principals demand accountability from the more powerful agent, and therefore, in the context of moral hazard, the accountability relationship aims to support the interests of the less powerful. The chapter explores accountability through this lens, addressing first horizontal accountability then vertical accountability. Horizontal accountability involves the relationship between institutions of *equal status*, typically state institutions of restraint, whereas vertical accountability refers to the state–citizen relationship, or the relationship between *unequals*. The critical literature on democratic accountability, state creation and taxation is drawn on to examine the relevance of this traditional approach towards vertical accountability.

Chapter 3 deconstructs procedural accountability and constructs relational accountability based on an interdisciplinary discussion drawing on economics, sociology, anthropology and philosophy. Perspectives on power are often implicit in theories of accountability, but here we make this explicit. We acknowledge that power is ubiquitous, dispersed, often subject-less, and can shape perceptions and views, therefore its application often does not emerge explicitly through conflict. We examine the location of the assumptions of accountability at different levels of analysis: from the individual to the institutional and the structural, and deconstruct the meaning of terms, including rationality, motivation, individuals (or actors), power, culture and society. At the level of the individual, we ask whether individuals are motivated by rational optimisations or whether altruism and morality influence behaviour, and, if so, from where such other influences may arise. We also deconstruct the concept of the actor, exploring the interrelationship between agency and structure. We develop a model of elites to see how they influence policies and decisions, linking the state and society and ensuring their own legitimacy. The reach of accountability stretches out in a fluid web-like structure, and continual contestation among elite factions functions through networks, which allow actors to move between factions and between positions. Here, we also review theories of the state and analyse how the state sits in relation to society.

Chapter 4 considers the conditionalities associated with aid, power relations and their influence. We discuss the impact that conditions associated with aid can have on the policy space of government, and that models of conditionality outline the different interests of donors and recipients in terms of whether there is conflict over preferences for reform. Recipient government capacity is typically limited and, therefore, through dependencies and transaction costs associated with the different aid modalities, aid financing can be accompanied by perverse incentives, with vested interests influencing resource allocations. This is framed in the context of dissonance between, on the one hand, events within the procedural tiers of the hierarchy and, on the other, the more pervasive higher-level relational characteristics. We discuss the foreign policy context and the international aid environment, and explore how different donors face different constraints which means that not all are constrained by the liberal model of democracy and good governance, although geopolitical concerns of security and protecting coalitions of investment are common to all. The rapid growth of finance from donors outside the Organisation for Economic Co-operation and Development's Development Assistance Committee, as well as expectations of future hydrocarbon revenues, are changing patterns of influence and negotiation and having a direct impact on the policy space for recipient governments. We argue that more explicit consideration of the political economy of donors and the constraints they face would allow expectations to be adjusted to more realistic levels.

Chapter 5 applies our model of accountability to Tanzania. We discuss the evolution of governmental institutions and agencies of the state and consider how they interact with society. We apply our understanding of the state and society from Chapter 3 to the historical and socio-political context in Tanzania, through an analysis of economic and political episodes in Tanzania's history. We see how the effectiveness of the leadership depends on the balance between the competing factions in relation to the dominant faction's ability to control power (Khan and Gray 2006). The need for resources to maintain stability has developed the relationship between political leaders and business leaders as political competition has increased. We explore how this has enabled political stability to be maintained through patron–client networks as politicians visibly deliver public goods to ensure votes, in explicit support of Chama Cha Mapinduzi's (CCM's) strategies. Local-level capture persists alongside this, and has the effect of maintaining individuals' positions of power. This sits within the realm of relational accountability, rather than with formal and contractual procedural accountability.

The allocative efficiency of public expenditure is likely reduced in several ways. For example, through a CCM vote-mobilisation strategy of providing visible public goods as welfare benefits that divert provision from less visible, but equally important, public goods. Another example is returning favours from private-sector actors, such as through the facilitation of tax evasion (which represents lost revenue), contract acquisition, or adjustments in the allocation of public goods. Finally local-level capture by politicians and local leaders, who provide goods to villages or wards, changes incentives for actors at the local level to find solutions for collective-action problems. The domination of the country by the same elite caucus for 50 years has been at the expense of civil society, which has been co-opted and restrained to maintain power. We see how the executive dominates in policy formulation and implementation and we analyse the limited influence of societal accountability. We consider how public financial management reforms have centralised the control of rents (Kelsall 2013), although challenges persist and the real influence happens during policy implementation processes, which is when effective 'policy' is actually determined and the influence of 'street-level bureaucrats' is exercised (Lipsky 2010, Kjær and Therkildsen 2013).

Chapter 6 focuses on the aid and accountability relationship in Tanzania and explores the rise and fall of general budget support. Although relational accountability differs in its epistemological roots from procedural accountability, we argue that the two coexist in the reality of the foreign-aid environment in Tanzania. This is by virtue of their location in different tiers of Williamson's framework, whereby relational accountability provides the framework within which procedural accountability can function. Here, we apply the new relational accountability framework from Chapter 3 in an analysis of the context of foreign aid in Tanzania. Aid is viewed from a broader perspective, understood to be greater than the sum of financial flows and associated conditionalities, and is seen as a pattern of social relations shaped by context and history. An outline of the recent history of aid provision to Tanzania presents the scale of aid and allows for an appreciation of its impact on the public finances. We consider the models of conditionality presented in Chapter 4, extending these to an exploration of the power relations and credibility issues associated with interactions between donors and the government. We analyse donor–government relations through the lenses of procedural and relational accountability, as well as the foreign policy context and the motivations of Tanzania and its donors in the international aid environment. We see how the increasing availability of finance from other donors without dialogue and conditionalities attached, as well as expectations of future hydrocarbon revenues, reduces the bargaining power of general budget support donors and increases the government's policy space. The relational notion of accountability places foreign aid in the context of the wider system, while considering how it is influenced by domestic politics. This chapter also describes the changing relationship with donors in the different periods of Tanzania's recent history. We see how procedural accountability is imposed as a tool by means of which donors understand the development context, an understanding embodied in monitoring and dialogue processes. However, its operation is tempered by the relational accountability context and methods. This has important implications for aid policy.

Chapter 7 concludes by highlighting the key aspects of procedural and relational accountability, distinguishing between the two and identifying their synergies and the symbiotic relationship we have uncovered. We summarise the case-study findings and discuss how a new approach to foreign aid would be beneficial. After this, we present policy recommendations that focus on the adoption of a new perspective that could effectively reduce the conflict between donors and government, and which has the potential to provide greater assistance in reforms and development. This revolves around adjusting the approach of donors to take into account the constraints associated with relational concerns, and deconstructing and recognising the accountability constraints on donors.

# Chapter 2

# Procedural Accountability:
# Necessary But Not Sufficient

## 2.1 Introduction

The traditional application and use of the term 'accountability' in public management, as applied in international development, is based on a principal–agent model that focuses on the contractual mechanisms for regulating behaviour between autonomous parties. Although accountability has been categorised in many ways, what is notable is the consistency of the underlying assumptions, which have remained fixed on notions of what motivates the principals and agents and on how to resolve the problems that arise in this relationship. It is a power relationship: one group of actors demands justification for the behaviour of another, and it is often the less powerful (the principal) who demands accountability from the more powerful (the agent). In the context of moral hazard, the accountability relationship aims to support the interests of the less powerful, who may be marginalised.

This chapter considers the dominance of traditional, or procedural, accountability by examining agencies of restraint and parliamentary democracy (Collier 1999, O'Donnell 1999), or the horizontal and vertical (H–V) accountability framework. The H–V framework was chosen to illustrate this discussion because most of the traditional notions of accountability can be found within this model: ranging from democracy linking state and society, to the role of state agencies in accountability. However, a number of different types of accountability have been defined and, while the H–V framework captures these, it also omits many important aspects, thereby allowing only a partial understanding. For example, it excludes the informal, the personal, the unspecified and unwritten aspects of behaviour, and the functioning of power and, therefore, the actual levels of complexity involved.

It is worth considering each aspect of procedural accountability in depth so as to be able to present a full picture of the H–V accountability framework. The next section draws on the critical literature on democratic accountability, state creation and taxation in order to further examine the relevance of the traditional approach to accountability.

## 2.2 Horizontal Accountability

We have defined the agents of horizontal accountability as agencies of state, including law courts, ombudspersons, audit offices, electoral tribunals and central banks. For their effective functioning, these have to have both the authority and the willingness 'to oversee, control, redress, and/or sanction unlawful actions of ... state agencies' (O'Donnell 1999: 39). While horizontal accountability requires a clear division of powers *between* state agencies, for such agencies to operate effectively they must also be part of a network, as they cannot operate in isolation. Such a network is based on relationships between both *equals* and *unequals*, which undermines the idea of a purely horizontal relationship between state agencies. The reality is therefore more complex.

Transparency is often mistaken for accountability, and, while it is necessary for accountability, it is not sufficient. The central bank literature on accountability (Castellani 2002, Castellani and Debrun 2005, De Haan et al. 1999, Eijffinger and Hoeberichts 2002, Ullrich 2003) highlights this distinction, identifying transparency as an element of accountability that enables evaluation of a central bank's performance through the availability of information. Castellani (2002) defines transparency as an *ex-ante* decision by a central bank for its communication strategy, and accountability as an *ex-post* political intervention.

We can break down the concept of transparency into five categories to highlight its different stages in the policymaking process. Political transparency relates to the motives of policymakers, including in terms of their policy objectives and institutional arrangements. Economic transparency speaks to the economic information used to develop policy. Procedural transparency describes the way policy decisions are made, including strategy, minutes and voting. Policy transparency involves announcements and explanations of policies. Finally, operational transparency refers to the implementation of policy (Geraats 2002).

While the basic horizontal-accountability model in the central bank literature is useful, its simplicity limits its applications. To increase its relevance to development discourse, we can introduce nuances, including the implications of the costs of accountability for its outcome, as well as with respect to power and collusion, in the cases of recursive and reciprocal accountability.

*Introducing Complexities: The Costs of Accountability*

Much of the literature does not take full account of the impact of the costs incurred by functioning accountability. Nor does it fully examine the case of a 'repeated game'.[1] For example, central banks being independent does not equate to them being accountable; a complex relationship exists between banks and government that has cost implications, as illustrated by Ullrich (2003). Where the choice of an inflation target makes the central bank's policies contestable, and different interest groups may attempt to gain influence, accountability is modelled in terms of expected losses accruing to government. These losses result from employing

---

1    Referring to game theory, which models the decisions of rational actors.

the instruments of accountability.[2] The decision on the introduction of an accountability mechanism is shown to be a direct function of the expected loss to the government in keeping the central bank accountable (2003).

This stresses the importance of calculating the costs of being accountable, and of understanding the effect these costs have on accountability outcomes. In the case of central banking, divergent interest groups have substantial impacts on costs, and, where a greater range of conflicting interest groups have an influence, the cost of negotiating an agreement will be higher (Ullrich 2003). The use of political institutions to achieve a negotiated agreement between the different interest groups is a major element of the cost of holding to account. The results show no clear-cut picture to indicate the choices of governments, but usefully highlight the complexities that governments face.

*Recursive and reciprocal accountability and other complexities*
Recursive and reciprocal accountability are among the variants of standard horizontal accountability and involve different types of relationships between the agencies involved. Reciprocal accountability exists when two agents 'check and balance' each other; recursive accountability is where A is accountable to B who is accountable to C, who is accountable to A (Schedler 1999: 26).

While agents and principals can be defined in relation to each other, it may be that, whereas principals demand accountability from agents, agents are in reality being accountable to other principals, active or not. This may be in pursuit of their own interests, or in response to more powerful interests. The challenge is to distinguish between the principal and the agent and their different motivations (Castellani and Debrun 2005). Conflicts arise between the central bank and the government as they each pursue their different goals. Furthermore, state agencies may collude with each other (Schmitter 1999). The risk of collusion creates a role for well-informed permanent agencies that have the power to challenge state agencies and that are accorded mutual recognition, even though they may not share the same legal status.

The horizontal-accountability framework can be extended to incorporate these variants, but the assumption that relationships are static persists, and the framework cannot easily address the potential for dynamic adjustments in accountabilities, or for overlapping accountabilities.

---

2    Ullrich uses the same instruments for holding the central bank accountable as Eijeffinger and Hoeberichts (replacement of the central banker; overriding of central bank decisions; and accountability to government). Ullrich's model differs from Eijeffinger and Hoeberichts's in two ways. First, she distinguishes between changing the decisions of the central bank in one isolated instance, and the *ex ante* abolishment of independence, or repeated overriding. Second, she assumes that independence is exogenous to the central bank and chosen by the government, as it is assumed to be difficult for the central bank to choose the optimal degree of independence.

Looking at the autonomy of *accountable* bodies from *accounting* bodies clarifies the challenge of defining horizontal accountability (Schedler 1999). To impose sanctions on the accountable party, the accounting party must be 'legally enabled and empowered' (O'Donnell 1999: 38). However, it is often the case that the former is more powerful than the latter. To deal with this difficulty, we propose using Schmitter's intermediate category of 'oblique accountability' (Schmitter 1999: 62): horizontal accountability here refers only to state actors; non-state actors operate within the realm of oblique accountability as they attempt to hold state agencies accountable.

Acknowledging these nuances means accepting a more complex and realistic picture of horizontal accountability than is commonly understood. The extent of accountability in the H–V model depends on the interaction between horizontal and vertical accountability, since accompanying weak horizontal accountability with strong vertical accountability will result in a different outcome. Can weak horizontal accountability be compensated for by vertical accountability (Bratton and Logan 2006)? We discuss this below before examining the limited explanatory power of the overall procedural accountability framework.

## 2.3  Vertical Accountability

Vertical accountability can be considered in terms of the relationship between unequals, such that the less powerful demand accountability from the more powerful (such as state agencies). Accountability can flow upwards or downwards; that is, vertical accountability can include both the demand for and the supply of accountability (Schedler 1999). By extension, the exercise of power can also flow in both directions: it flows downwards when higher-ranking public officials (principals) control their lower-ranking subordinates (agents); or upwards, implying that agents in society may hold some power.

Next, we explore the procedural notions of democratic accountability and taxation, and consider an international perspective. Democracy is a common theme in vertical accountability. Within the H–V framework, it is the main transmission mechanism by which accountability is considered to work. It is to the theories of democratic accountability, and to nuances such as power structures, information asymmetry and time inconsistency, that we now turn.

*Democratic Accountability*

We have already seen how accountability is much broader than the political system, but accountability discourse is commonly associated with democratic accountability and representation, which are mechanisms through which agents can control the actions of those to whom power has been delegated (Goetz and Jenkins 2005). Next, we consider analyses of democracy that fit within the procedural understanding of accountability, extending the model as far as possible without overriding the underlying economic assumptions of the framework, including that of rationality. Using literature that considers the political realities in developing countries, including neo-patrimonial politics, we then point out some limitations of the model.

Attempts to define the nature of democracy and, by extension, government, move us towards a classification for democracy. Sklar (1986) identifies five different types of democracy: liberal democracy; guided democracy; participatory democracy; consociational democracy;[3] and social democracy, for which he cites the example of Tanzania. Political competition underlies the definition of democracy. The different types of democracy can be seen as the operation of political competition, to differing extents based on the existence of different types of attribute, including alternative information, freedom of expression, associational autonomy and freedom of elected officials (Dahl 1989, O'Donnell 1999).

Considering the interrelationship between democracy and nation states, Grant and Keohane (2005) propose two models that highlight differences in who demands accountability. In the participatory model, those directly affected evaluate those holding power; in the delegation model, authority to undertake the evaluation is granted to trustees, who carry out evaluations on behalf of others. In reality, there may be a mixture of the two models in place. The delegation model, which most closely captures the relationship between the state and the electorate, operates most restrictively in a principal–agent format; in a trustee format, the power holder has more discretion. The principal–agent format requires that the leader directly follow the wishes of the electorate, and there is no scope for defying the popular will. In the trustee format, the agent may act out of line with the desires of the principal, but this could be justified as legitimate if it is shown to fulfil the terms of office.

What strategies might politicians use to gain votes? They might apply two different forms of representation: *representation as promising*, and *anticipatory representation* (Mansbridge 1998), both of which highlight the time inconsistency that exists between politicians and voters. *Representation as promising* involves politicians making promises during election campaigning to attract votes, with sanctions for non-delivery given at the next election. However, in reality, the short-term nature of politics, from the perspective of both the electorate and the politicians, makes the occurrence of such sanctions unlikely. *Anticipatory representation* involves politicians considering the preferences the electorate is likely to hold by the next election and actively attempting to shape these; a temporal that undermines accountability.

While useful, these concepts overlook the complexities of reality. As research from the Africa Power and Politics Programme has suggested, 'in its *current* form, democracy ... is, at best, a weak source of pressure for performance if top-down

---

3    Lijphart coined this term to refer to a type of liberal democracy that protects the interests of particular groups, for instance, in a divided society (1969). It would involve full representation of the main groups and voluntary cooperation among the elites and, therefore, is considered to be limited in reach in developing countries, including Africa (Sklar 1986).

disciplines are absent. At worst, it has helped to excuse or legitimise rule-breaking by officials and/or non-enforcement of rules by officials' (Booth 2012: 43, emphasis in original). As with horizontal accountability, we here develop nuances of vertical accountability – elements such as time inconsistency, information asymmetry and power relations – to present a fuller model of traditional accountability.

*Introducing Complexities*

For democracy to promote accountability effectively, voters need to be provided with a choice through a credible opposition party, and to be able to punish and reward politicians effectively (Jelmin 2012, Weghorst and Lindberg 2010). In reality, these requirements for democracy are not present (Jelmin 2012), and downward accountability through elections has been found not to compensate for the absence of top-down disciplines where strong leadership both demands and supports the delivery of public goods (Booth 2012, McCourt 2012).

There is a need to look beyond elections, as evidenced by our discussion of earlier definitions of vertical accountability (Dahl 1989, O'Donnell 1999, Sklar 1986). Concentrating on electoral activities can result in a narrow focus on peak periods of interaction between actors and the state, and in overlooking more frequent inter-electoral political activities. We need to redress this balance by considering the inter-temporal aspect of accountability, and the long-term gains that may be reaped through unpopular short-term policies. This raises questions as to the time period over which accountability should be applied (Mehta 2003, cited in Goetz and Jenkins 2005: 12). This also captures an inherent problem of democracy: the electoral cycle. The very nature of democracy requires that elections take place, but they can distort the nature of accountability and are highly dependent on information asymmetry.

Varying degrees of political participation exist between elections, with different behaviour patterns linked to wealth. Bratton and Logan (2006) find that poorer people are more likely to participate in elections and to participate in political activities between elections.

The calculus of reciprocity operating around democracy in clientelistic societies has implications for the delivery of public goods where strong top-down disciplines are absent, to summarise a wealth of important literature. Democracy may increase the provision of some public goods and reduce the provision of others, because the types of goods and services that are allocated to obtain political support relate to the association of the good or service with the politician (Booth 2012, Harding and Wantchekon 2010, Mcloughlin and Batley 2012). The political currency of the provision may be increased by five characteristics: 1) as the visibility of the goods increases (Mani and Mukland 2007); 2) where the goods' simplicity increases the politicians' ability to claim credit for their provision (World Bank 2003); 3) where they are consumed individually, how they are targeted towards users (Keefer and Khemani 2003); 4) where they are heavily demanded (Water and Sanitation

Programme 2011); or 5) where demand is linked to specific characteristics such as language and culture in the provision of education (Pritchett 2002).

So far, this discussion has involved an unidentified voter, who has been presented as being homogenous and unified, and an electoral candidate. The reality is, of course, much more complex, as there are many more actors involved, on the sides of both those representing the electorate and those being represented. For instance, for those representing, conflicting mandates may reduce the ability of the elected legislator to be accountable; in addition to being responsive to the electorate, they have to respond to the demands of the party, or even funders (Mejía Acosta 2013).

Unsurprisingly, voters hold inaccurate beliefs about both the policy impact and the policy context in relation to redistributive issues (Taylor-Gooby et al. 2003). Information asymmetry skews the relationship between democratic representation and democratic accountability, as voters are not fully aware of government decisions, policy choices and likely outcomes. Indeed, the functioning of political parties is such that voters are presented with a limited range of policy choices. This is exacerbated by the electoral cycle, as periodic elections present a temporal element to information asymmetry, such that information differs over time. Different political behaviour patterns and demands for vertical accountability are also linked to wealth. Bratton and Logan (2006) find that poorer people are less likely to consider they are *receiving* democracy from their government, as poorer citizens have lower expectations of their right to demand accountability and a low perception that accountability is being delivered, with politicians perceived to renege on their promises.

What role might anticipation play in voting activity? Voters' actions are not based simply on accountability to an existing or past government, but are instead a reflection of the anticipated behaviour of a political party in terms of its ability to be an effective government (Fearon 1999, Keefer 2007, Keefer and Khemani 2005). As voters understand that the circumstances under which policy is made change from mandate to mandate, representation is therefore anticipatory. We can extend this to the function of populism in politics and the personalisation of both the politician and the voter. Rather than being based on individual choice or consideration of policies, voting is a 'calculus of patrimonial reciprocity based on ties of solidarity', according to Chabal and Daloz (1999: 39). Here, the motivation to vote comes from an expectation that they should be seen to vote in a particular way, and leaders are never to be separated from their supporters: 'They remain directly linked to them through a myriad of nepotistic or clientelistic networks staffed by dependent intermediaries' (1999).[4] At all times, leaders must be seen as catering to those on whom their political legitimacy rests.

Voters are individual actors who exist within society, but they may also be represented by social movements and organisations. These organisations themselves have to be legitimised, although their sources of legitimacy are different and are

---

4   This is considered further in the discussion of power in Chapter 3.

intertwined with the responsiveness of state institutions: for example, freedom of speech and information and the right to demonstrate (Jelmin 2012). Civil-society organisations are subject to the same representation critiques as political parties, as they are also subjected to inequalities of power; furthermore, they are rarely subject to internal democratic process, and many represent specific interests that benefit small groups of people, may be co-opted by funders, and often have little accountability to their members (Jelmin 2012, Rocha Menocal and Sharma 2008). Chapter 3 further explores what we mean by society, and how the individual actor both forms and reacts to this.

In this discussion, we have outlined the concept of democracy as it is used within the procedural understanding of accountability, and have extended it to include inter-electoral activities, information asymmetry and time inconsistency. It is possible to critique this understanding through the incorporation of clientelism and by considering networks of reciprocity that remove the separation between voters and electoral candidates. Both of these prevent the operation of the traditional form of accountability. Rather than a model of government that is ethical and efficient and requires merely being held to account by principals in order to deliver, this understanding indicates a model where the government is responding to other incentives and faces its own costs and challenges, beyond being elected. The traditional notion of accountability cannot capture the resulting behaviour of governmental actors, limiting the usefulness of the concept of procedural accountability.

Underpinning these theories of democracy are notions of the state and the citizen–state relationship. This hinges on the tax state (Schumpeter 1918,1991), whereby tax payments are seen as payment for political influence through voting during elections. Therefore, we now turn to ask how taxation operates within the procedural framework of vertical accountability.

*Taxation and Accountability: Collective Action and State Creation*

In this section, we review theories of collective action and collective bargaining. We also look at theories of state creation and the emergence of the social contract, and how this is underpinned by theories of citizenship. The political context in Africa differs in comparison with that noted in the early literature on developing Europe, presenting a different background against which different collective identities could emerge. Both the literature and the empirical evidence highlight the impact of different types of taxes on accountability, and of the differing nature of the taxation system on the outcome. The debate on the impact of taxation on vertical accountability is based on the historical experience of today's developed countries that taxation has increased the vertical accountability of the state to its constituency (Tilly 1992).

*Collective action*

As outlined in Chapter 1, the problem of collective action underpins the entire discussion around accountability. Collective action describes local organisation to solve problems, through the development of rules or institutions, which is underpinned by 'consent, trust and legitimacy', and rests upon citizens accepting the limits to their individual actions in favour of collective representation (Daunton 2001, with reference to taxation). Applying this to accountability, taxation and the state, the fiscal constitution and public choice address this. First, the fiscal constitution, based on J.S. Mill's Representative Government (1861), involves the creation of rules and procedures resulting in constitutional upper limits on the amount of tax the state can extract. The fiscal constitution forms the parameters within which disputes take place, and is itself periodically renegotiated. Second, public-choice models assume individuals make rational choices based on the maximisation of utility, and on a coercive relationship between the state and the individual. These assumptions do not take into account the complexity of motivations, and ignore the ways in which collective action can emerge.

Within the public-choice school, Bates and Lien (1985) find that the emergence of collective groups referred to in the writings about early European history owed to the savings for monarchs when bargaining with groups rather than with individuals. As the costs of arriving at a collective agreement were lower and the benefits were higher, bargaining took place on a collective level, preventing defection of payment and therefore resulting in a higher tax yield for the monarch. From the perspective of the taxpayer, this reduced the opportunities to free-ride, because, once tax institutions were established, their rules were soon universally applied. This prevented the emergence of jealousies and conflicts.

How can we understand accountability in the reality of overlapping and contradictory responsibilities and allegiances? Considering the behavioural basis for collective action helps us do this by extending the public-choice theory to one of bounded rationality, focusing on the emergence of norms of trust and the psychological basis for decision making. For collective action to arise and, for example, society to demand accountability, a desire and the opportunity for political organisation are necessary.

The balance of identities at any point in time is a function of the particular circumstances, and building up large support networks (or a 'circle of trust') is important (Chabal and Daloz 1999: 27). This hints at the existence of the complex nature of collective action. One person can move from dominating in one situation to being dominated in another, and it may be that someone's short-term interests differ from their long-term interests. It should not be assumed that social actors have 'an uncomplicated interest in better governance and better public services' (Booth 2012: 70) as these complexities may not translate into incentives for improved public goods. It also depends on initial levels of cooperation: if these are positive and high, trust may build up as actors learn to rely on one another, and as trustworthy reputations become self-reinforcing. Therefore, structural variables are related to a 'triangle of trust, reciprocity' and reputation', which have an impact on levels of cooperation (Ostrom 1998: 13).

Chapter 3 develops this further by considering the reality of the political economy context in developing countries, discussing a more complex and dynamic picture of accountability.

*Theories of state creation*

A social contract is a contractual relationship between citizens and the state that involves collective representation to overcome the problem of collective action. Citizenship describes the social contract, or 'the roles and responsibilities of the state, as well as the rights and entitlements of citizens' and forms the basis against which accountability claims can be made (Newell and Wheeler 2006: 29). However, the literature on state building and donor support has emphasised the state, and increasing its capacity, rather than attempting to give the social actor an equal, or at least, a sufficient role in holding the state accountable (by developing relationships between individuals in society and the state) (Eyben and Ladbury 2006).

Having discussed collective action and considered the degree to which procedural accountability is a helpful framework for understanding the realities of collective action, we now consider whether and how social contract theories, as applied in the accountability literature, depend on both the structure of taxation and theories of collective action.

A wealth of literature supports the relationship between the state and taxation (Bates 2001, Bates 2007, Bates and Lien 1985, Levi 1988, Mann 1993, Moore 2001, Moore 2004a, Moore 2004b, Moore 2007a, Moore 2007b, North 2004, North 2005, Olson 1965, Schumpeter 1918 1991, Skocpol 1992, Tilly 1992). It deals with the recompensing of paid taxes through the offer of political influence via elections; consensual taxation, involving the exchange of revenues in return for policies (Moore 2004a; Moore 2004b); and the creation of an incentive for rulers to respond by delivering services to retain their power.

Since the beginnings of the state, it is relevant to consider whether there was always a relationship between the state and citizens through taxation or whether there was a different context before taxation. In order to explore this, we need to consider the social contract on which the relationship between the citizen and the state came to be based. This concept first emerged with Hobbes' Leviathan (1651, 1909) and Grotius (1625), who believed individuals had to give away their rights to an absolute regime, which arose through a turning point: a state of war or fear. Locke (1689) and Rousseau (1762), in contrast, considered human rights to be natural rights that could not be alienated and that a ruler could not take absolute authority; rather, a political process takes place whereby citizens' quasi-voluntary compliance (Levi 1988) permits state legitimacy (Bird et al. 2004). Extrapolating from this, such compliance with the state requires that the taxation system sufficiently represents the basic values of a proportion of the population, determined by the balance between the importance of taxation and other policy issues for which individuals vote via the democratic system.[5]

Critics of social contract theory argue that almost all citizens grow up within an existing society, and therefore never have a choice as to whether to enter into a social contract. The question then becomes how the social contract is *maintained*, and how it *evolves* during times of change. Another criticism of social contract theory is that it relies on elections to provide governments with the mandate for taxation, which subsequently allows the development of the contract, and it is therefore subject to the weaknesses identified below.

1. Taxpayers have insufficient information to know whether the bargain has been sufficiently met.
2. Elections are seen to play a pivotal role in downplaying the influence of other aspects that have an impact on any contractual relationship. In reality, constraints such as information asymmetry, time inconsistency and limited choice prevents voters from being able to select their ideal choice of representative through elections.
3. While it seems that elections provide a range of policy choices from which the electorate can choose, in reality, political parties present very limited policy choices to voters.
4. Patronage relations are not regarded as important.

In developing Britain, a parliament was in existence prior to the emergence of the social contract. This represented overseas traders and large taxpayers, who were brought into negotiation by the British elite, often in secrecy. This resulted in the influence of interest groups being limited and increased power being accorded to a small group of politicians (Daunton 2001). Although many of today's developing countries have legislatures that *appear* to be representative, with extensive fiscal powers, and many have established forums for negotiation between taxpayers and the government, we cannot ignore the powerful interest groups that serve well-established clientelistic interests, just as they did in developing Britain. Key issues to consider include the balance between powerful groups; the extent of

---

5    Historically, the way in which taxation was extracted was a function of the relationship between the state and citizens, and the resultant revenue affected the capacity of the state. One such characteristic is the extent of negotiation or coercion in the system and any resulting tensions: the examples of Britain and France are illustrative in this regard (Bates and Lien 1985: 7, Daunton 2001: 5, Moore 2004a: 302, Ormrod et al. 1999, Sussman 2005). The factors underlying the creation of the British fiscal state include changes in the structure of the economy, which allowed for increased revenue collections; and the instigation of the parliamentary and administrative system, which permitted negotiation and resulted in the move to a consensual tax system. This is in contrast with greater resistance in France, where fewer opportunities for bargaining and more visible exemptions resulted in 'local and sectoral opposition', which constrained the system (Daunton 2001: 7, Sussman 2005).

bias and capture involved; and the role these play in the accountability of today's developing country governments. Such considerations are outside the scope of procedural accountability.

We have reviewed the background to theories of state creation and the formation of the social contract on which the procedural notion of vertical accountability rests. Having explored how collective representation may have arisen in a move towards a tax state – as well as the limitations of this – we now turn to taxation and accountability, which are key aspects of the procedural notion of vertical accountability.

*Taxation and accountability*
The complexities of collection action and the limitations in applying the theory of state creation to sub-Saharan Africa present serious problems for the particular relationship between taxation and accountability that is implied by the vertical-accountability model. In sub-Saharan Africa, the structure of taxes does not align with that expected by procedural accountability, where theories of state creation require that the tax burden be felt by citizens. Instead, the predominantly indirect nature of taxation in sub-Saharan Africa weakens the accountability relationship, as defined by the H–V framework: citizens do not *feel* the tax burden as explicitly related to services they receive. It matters not only what the tax levels are, but also how the tax level has been chosen, how it is imposed and how the funds are used (Bird et al. 2004).

The composition of taxes is linked closely to the stage of development, and low-income countries typically rely heavily on customs. Their revenues are therefore constrained by their performance in external markets. A reason for this is that, in the early stages of development, other sources of revenue have not been developed, and, as trade taxes are simple and easy to collect, they dominate as a revenue source (Farhadian-Lorie and Katz 1989). The tax structure in developing Europe differs from that in sub-Saharan Africa. In low-income African countries, outside the oil-producing countries, where direct taxes dominate, there is a dominance of indirect taxes (Leuthold 1991).[6] Developing countries raise much more from corporate income tax than from individual income tax (Tanzi 1992): 2 per cent of gross domestic product and 1.1 per cent, respectively, between 1978 and 1988. If the social contract accountability perspective is held, this pattern limits the accountability-building influence of taxation (Brautigam 2002, Ghura 1998, Gloppen and Rakner 2002, Moss and Subramanian 2005).

Willingness to pay tax depends on the perception that government institutions are honest and responsive, as corruption and the rule of law are found to play important roles in determining tax collections (Bird et al. 2004).[7] Dictatorships and

---

6    Indirect taxes are defined as value-added tax and other sales taxes and customs and excise taxes. Direct taxes are those imposed directly on a person or company, such as income tax and corporation tax.

7    Bird et al. analysed a sample of 110 developing and transitional countries.

coercive authorities can collect taxes through forcible extraction (Haggard 1990, cited in Cheibub 1998, Fjeldstad 2001); here, the absence of the need to gain electoral approval provides an important additional degree of freedom for coercive taxation (Cheibub 1998).

## *A Further Complexity: International Accountability*

The discussion above focused on procedural accountability in the national context. Placing the accountability relationship in the international context has the potential to change the balance of power between the principal and the agent. Using the example of donors and recipient governments, the asymmetry in the power relationship increases, as accountability becomes distributed across a range of organisations and actors, through network governance. Elected leaders can use this dynamic to sidestep public debate (Krahmann 2002, cited in Goetz and Jenkins 2005: 23), and therefore the power of donors to demand accountability from recipients may reduce. This is a missing dimension in conventional discussions of accountability: international accountability (Pastor 1999).

The most relevant aspects of accountability in the context of international politics – with regard to aid – are fiscal accountability, peer accountability and public reputational accountability. Hierarchical, supervisory fiscal and legal mechanisms that rely on democratic delegation are most relevant in understanding traditional accountability in the public sector.

Hierarchical accountability is found in bureaucracies and characterises relationships within organisations, such as the Tanzanian public service, where it is maintained through adjustments in remuneration, responsibilities and career opportunities. Supervisory accountability concerns relationships between organisations, such as those between the World Bank and the courts and states that oversee its work. Fiscal accountability concerns the relationship between a funder and a recipient, in which the funder can demand financial reports and has the power to sanction the recipient (Grant and Keohane 2005; see Table 2.1). This can be seen as a 'soft' form of conditionality, in which compliance with donor reporting procedures is required. This compliance itself means that opportunities are lost to consider challenges in a way that may lead to thinking about collective action challenges, and facilitating their solutions (Booth 2012). Legal accountability involves the operation of accountability through the trustee model of democracy, resorting to formal rules, against which actions may be justified (Grant and Keohane 2005, see Table 2.1).

Sitting within the participatory model of democracy, the final two categories are of relevance in relation to the accountability of budget support: peer accountability and public reputational accountability. Peer accountability involves the evaluation of one organisation by another, most commonly of non-governmental organisations by their counterparts in government. Finally, public reputational accountability – the accountability of organisation or institutions to public opinion – can be found

**Table 2.1     Seven mechanisms of international accountability in world politics**

| Mechanism | Accountability holder | Power wielder | Cost to power wielder | Example |
|---|---|---|---|---|
| Hierarchical | Leaders of organisation | Subordinate official | Loss of career opportunities | Authority of United Nations Secretary-General |
| Supervisory | States | Multilateral organisation and its executive head | Restraints on ability to act, loss of office | World Bank and International Monetary Fund: governance by their executive boards |
| Fiscal | Funding agencies | Funded agency | Budget restrictions | Withholding of United Nations dues |
| Legal | Courts | Individual official or agency | From restriction of authority to criminal penalties | International Criminal Court |
| Market | Equity and bond holders and consumers | Firm or government | Loss of access to, or higher cost of capital | Refusal of capital markets to finance developing country governments during world financial crises |
| Peer | Peer organisations | Organisations and their leaders | Effects on network ties and therefore on others' support | The evaluation by an independent marine-certification body of a Greenpeace–Shell controversy |
| Public reputational* | Peers and diffuse public | Individual or agency | Diffuse effects on reputation, prestige, self-esteem | Effects on United States 'soft power' of unilateralism |

*Note:* *Reputational effects are involved in all issues of accountability, as mechanisms leading to punishment through hierarchy, supervision, fiscal measures, legal action, the market and peer responses. The category of reputational effects refers to situations where the other means of accountability are not available.

*Source:* Adapted from Grant, R.W., and R.O. Keohane. 2005. Accountability and Abuses of Power in World Politics. *The American Political Science Review* 99 (1):29–43. Page: 36, Table 2.

in many of the mechanisms, but it can also exist when they are not present, and operates as a 'soft' power, the shaping of the preferences of others (Nye 2008: 95).[8]

The operation of transparency is particularly important for those mechanisms that are based on participatory democracy: market, peer and reputational accountability. These mechanisms cannot function if information is not freely and widely available. This is also true of democratic accountability within states where the supervisory role operates, as, in order for the supervision to take place, information must be freely available. While transparency may be at the root of these mechanisms, and may be the easiest component of accountability (as discussed in relation to horizontal accountability), it is not sufficient: 'Without standards and sanctions and a configuration of power that enables sanctions to be imposed relatively consistently on all violators of standards – accountability that is both effective and widely viewed as legitimate will remain elusive' (Grant and Keohane 2005: 40).

The type of accountability in operation thus depends on the strength of the state. For instance, a weak and dependent state, as found in countries reliant on foreign aid, is fiscally accountable and supervised by international organisations, and by its donor states. It is more likely that a weak state will experience a crisis resulting in the delegation of authority to an international organisation. For example, in the event of a financial crisis, a weak state might delegate authority to the International Monetary Fund. There may, of course, be an element of evasion of accountability in this. As states increase in strength, they come across more negotiation constraints, as they attempt to obtain cooperation from, and influence, other states. The greater the involvement of states in interdependent networks, the greater the complexity of competing perspectives, and therefore, the more constraints are faced in reaching settlements (Grant and Keohane 2005).

As complexities of interdependence, networks and the personalised nature of relationships between the representatives of countries and international organisations are added to the model, procedural accountability becomes weaker in terms of its explanatory power.

### 2.4 Summary: Procedural Accountability Re-examined

In this chapter, we have discussed the traditional concept of accountability through an examination of the H–V accountability framework, and have extended this model through the inclusion of nuances (such as the costs of accountability and recursive and reciprocal accountability, including power disparities). In exploring horizontal accountability, we have analysed the accountability that institutions of equal status impose on each other, outlined the distinction between accountability and transparency and the different stages of transparency in the policymaking process, as well as defined the specific mechanisms of accountability.

---

8  Chapter 3 will discuss the conceptualisations of power in detail.

The extension of the simple horizontal-accountability model to consider the costs associated with accountability, and the complexities of recursive and reciprocal accountability, including power and collusion, has been discussed. Collusion blurs the lines between the principal and the agent, presenting enforcement difficulties (Castellani and Debrun 2005, Schmitter 1999). We have argued that the model is too simplistic. Even though it can be extended to cover recursive accountability, it struggles with the possibility of dynamic recursive accountability, and with overlapping accountabilities, as not only may state agencies collude with each other but alliances may also be dynamic and overlapping, rather than simply static.

In terms of vertical accountability – the relationship between unequals – we have focused on democratic accountability, taxation and international accountability; issues of power and information asymmetries; and the realities of social and political structures. The literature widely criticises the concept of democratic accountability (and, by extension, vertical accountability) for being oversimplified and for not capturing the complexities of reality. Nuances, such as time inconsistency, information asymmetry, and power relations are crucial to presenting a fuller model of traditional accountability. However, the models are still unable to explain the political reality in many developing countries, where clientelist politics is prevalent.

Rather than the homogeneous economic actor with a predetermined utility function, which procedural accountability implies, the reality in many developing countries is that of a fragmentation of identities, with each individual having a variety of different identities. These complexities require that we move away from the simple principal–agent framework to consider the reality, where it is not simply the rulers versus the ruled. Relations are dynamic and often inconsistent, as one person can move from dominating in one situation to being dominated in another, or someone's short-term interests can differ from their long-term interests.

In the new context of complexity, we have asked what the relationship is between the state and its citizens. The social contract requires that the taxation system adequately represents the values of a proportion of the population, and therefore depends on theories of both taxation and democracy. Many of today's developing countries have legislatures that *appear* to be representative; however, underneath this, there are powerful interest groups operating, serving well-established political settlements and clientelistic interests. Moving beyond the scope of procedural accountability, pertinent issues include the balance between powerful groups with allegiances to the state; the extent of bias and capture involved; and the role such issues play in the accountability context.

The underlying assumptions of public management permeate the procedural accountability model. These include the assumption of rational principals, and agents who are maximising their own individual interests, which aggregate linearly to an outcome for society as a whole. In response to this, contractual mechanisms for regulating behaviour between autonomous parties are employed, leading to the assumptions that accountability is measurable and identifiable, and allows for the adoption of predictable solutions. Behaviour and results that fall outside this understanding have a negative value judgement placed upon them, and are considered detrimental. The fundamental weaknesses in the models of H–V and procedural accountability – including the complexity of the network of accountability, and the personal nature of the accountability within patronage relationships – highlight the need to reconsider how accountability functions.

Chapter 3 pursues these criticisms through an analysis of the concepts implicit in the traditional notion of accountability. It deconstructs in detail the assumptions underlying the procedural understanding of accountability, and presents the more complex picture, which has been touched on in this Chapter, of relational accountability: a complementary concept that, when considered alongside procedural accountability, allows for a full understanding of how accountability operates in practice. We explore the limitations to the concept of rationality, moving to consider: bounded rationality, the emergence of norms of trust, and psychological bases for decision making. This will enable the emergence of an understanding of accountability that is less procedural in nature, and more complex, with overlapping and potentially contradictory responsibilities and allegiances.

# Chapter 3
# Relational Accountability: the Missing Component

## 3.1 Introduction

Building on the deconstruction of the procedural understanding of accountability in Chapter 2, this chapter develops a theory of the state and society so as to be able to move towards a new and complete model of accountability.

Chapter 2 discussed the traditional, or procedural, model of accountability through a presentation of the horizontal–vertical (H–V) framework, analysing accountability relations within, and between, state institutions (horizontal accountability) and between the state and society (vertical accountability). Despite the limitations of the procedural model, it has come to dominate international relations as part of the public management ethos. It is based on a number of assumptions rooted in a rationalist economic epistemology, including that rational principals operate to maximise their own individual interests. This implicit epistemology assumes certain international best practices and standards, as well as certain motivations of actors and agencies (Gulrajani 2010).

In this chapter, we deconstruct each element of the traditional procedural notion of accountability and extend the understanding of accountability to become relational, through an interdisciplinary discussion that draws on economics, sociology, anthropology, political theory and philosophy.

We examine where the assumptions of accountability lie, and their theoretical roots at different levels: the individual, the institutional and the structural. This allows for the deconstruction of terms such as 'power', 'rationality', 'motivation', 'individuals' (or 'actors'), 'culture' and 'society'. At the level of the individual, we ask whether people are motivated merely by rational optimisations and find that there are other influences on behaviour such as altruism and morality. In deconstructing these terms we can begin to consider where these influences on behaviour, other than pure maximisation, come from. We also look at the concept of the actor: who are the motivated individuals or actors? And what is their influence on units of economic and social organisation?

We examine the interaction between these different factors: between the individual and the economic unit, organisation or institution; and, temporally, between the behavioural outcome and the influence on future behaviour. We then go on to explore the interrelationship between agency and structure, and consider how the highly embedded relational context centres on clientelistic relations that are often based on informal rules that involve retaining the 'circle of trust' or supporting networks of elites.

We also discuss the evolution of governmental institutions and agencies of the state and how they interact with society. This enables an enhanced understanding of what accountability means, and allows a distinction to be made between traditional and rationalist understandings of accountability (procedural accountability) on one hand, and a more realistic understanding of accountability (relational accountability) on the other. Although relational accountability differs in its epistemological roots from procedural accountability, the two can coexist by virtue of their location in different levels of Williamson's hierarchy of social analysis (discussed in Chapter 1), whereby relational accountability provides the framework within which procedural accountability can function. This understanding of the state and society forms the basis for the discussion of the historical and sociopolitical context in Tanzania in Chapter 5. In this chapter we start with a discussion of power and how it is used to influence. Often implicit, this is made explicit to develop our concept of relational accountability.

### 3.2  Power and Influence

The role of power is implicit in models of accountability; it is the basis of both the relationship between aid donors and governments, and the relationship between the state and society. Indeed, in Chapter 2 we define accountability as involving a power relationship: one group of actors demands justification for the behaviour of another group, and it is often the less powerful (principal) who demands accountability from the more powerful (agent).

It is necessary to consider what is meant by power, as it is a term that is laden with implicit values: 'both its very definition and any given use of it, once defined, are inextricably tied to a given set of (probably unacknowledged) value-assumptions which predetermine the range of its empirical application' (Lukes 1974, 2005: 30). In this discussion of power we aim to explicitly frame how it is applied in this book, rather than attempting to do justice to the wealth of fascinating analyses of power.

We have seen that procedural accountability invokes a simple power relationship, where the less powerful (principal) demands accountability from the more powerful (agent); in the presence of moral hazard, the accountability relationship supports the interests of the less powerful. While Chapter 2 extends the model of procedural accountability to include a number of complexities, the model remains rooted in decision-making and non-decision-making power as a limited and constrained resource (Lukes' (2005) first and second dimensions of power, discussed below).

The perspective on power that we apply fundamentally differs from that implicit in procedural accountability. Here we see power as ubiquitous and dispersed. While present at both the level of the individual and in social structures it is often enacted within strategies that do not have individual authors; it is latent as it is a capacity that need not be enacted. Power is a fluid process that emerges in ideologies, it has an implicit role in shaping perceptions and views to the extent that people do not necessarily recognise the sources of their beliefs: it works 'against people's interests by misleading them, thereby distorting their judgement' (Lukes 1974, 2005: 14, applying Bourdieu's concept of 'habitus'). In short, power is considered an implicit process at play in all relations and used specifically to co-opt and to strengthen associations within networks (Murdoch and Marsden 1995). Power is therefore also firmly present within accountability relationships. The concept of procedural accountability cannot, however, be sufficiently expanded to incorporate power as ubiquitous and a capacity that influences all social and economic interactions. To overcome this weakness we apply a relational conceptualisation of power that arises from the specific political and cultural history.

Foucault's work has been important in shaping views of power as pervasive and diffuse and of 'constitut[ing] agents rather than being deployed by them' (Gaventa 2003: 3). Foucault (1979) claims that the production of knowledge provides a structure for power. This is done by positioning people as subjects and using knowledge as power through technology, most commonly through the dominant discipline of science where perspectives are presented as 'truths'. Foucault's work on the use of power for punishment in prisons, from which he draws commonalities with other institutions, identifies 'normalizing judgements' as an instrument of disciplinary power (Foucault 1979: 183). This sees behaviour as being judged in terms of the dominant norm and a corresponding punishment being administered if the norm is violated. This is clearly relevant for accountability, as it involves standards, evaluation and sanctions. However, alongside this explicit contestation, Foucault also emphasises the more covert operation of power through hegemony, as values are adjusted to incorporate beliefs. Indeed, it can be argued that the application of procedural accountability is covert, as it implies a latent set of beliefs that overlooks the wider social context in which relational accountability operates.

Lukes (1974, 2005) identified three dimensions of power which are useful to distinguish the different assumptions about power that are applied in the procedural and relational conceptualisations of accountability. The first dimension of power builds on the work of Dahl (1957, 1958, 1968) and Polsby (1963). This sees power as being visible through conflicts of interests that are focussed on behaviour in decision making (Lukes 2005). This first dimension is critiqued for emphasising 'initiating, deciding, and vetoing' and situates power in the operation of 'safe' issues (Bachrach and Baratz 1970: 6). The second dimension therefore extends the first dimension to include non-decision making. In doing so, it allows voices to be kept covert through power. The third dimension is the one that we are most interested in here. It allows for the presence of 'latent conflict' where there is 'a contradiction between the interests of those exercising power and the *real* interests of those they exclude'. (Lukes 2005: 28 [original emphasis]).

We can describe power from the perspective of the citizen through empowerment. Accountability is demanded through participation and the exercising of voice. Outcomes often reflect the relative social, political and economic opportunities of actors (Goetz and Jenkins 2001, Gaventa 2006, Just Associates 2007). These are complex and dynamic and it may be that formal rules sit in tension with informal rules (O'Neill, Foresti and Hudson 2007). Here power can be seen as the degree to which actors are empowered to effectively contest the norms that are dominant in society.

Khan (1996a, 1996b) claims the power distribution in society has a major impact on corruption which, in turn, is influenced by a country's specific political and cultural history. This is located within the relational Level 1 of Williamson's hierarchy (see Figure 1.2). The arrangement of power in a society has been categorised by two types of patron–client networks: clientelistic and patrimonial. The distinction between the two is rooted in the differing legitimacy of the state. In the patrimonial network, the state does not face constraints in the allocation of resources. In clientelistic contexts, clients are often more powerful such that they can impose constraints on the state; with payoffs from the state reflecting the relative power of clients (Khan 2004a). The clientelistic and patrimonial networks are both characterised by patterns of power that allow the patron to distribute resources to the client; blurred boundaries between the public and private; and an informalisation where formal rules are not seen as important (Chabal and Daloz 1999, Bratton and Van de Walle 1997, Jackson and Rosberg 1982, Médard 1982).

While we use the broader term clientelism in this discussion, our focus is often on a specific type of clientelism: prebendalism. Prebendalism impacts a smaller number of people in mainly symbolic, rather than redistributive, ways, as it involves fewer resources. Typically emerging from a context of limited development and a history of authoritarian rule – where the focus is on the achievement of political power and stability – state offices are appropriated and exploited for private gain (Joseph 1988, 2012, Van de Walle 2007).

## 3.3 State and Society

This chapter discusses what we understand by the terms 'state' and 'society', so we can explicitly examine the units of analyses underpinning the development of relational accountability. Whereas Chapter 2 explored the state institutions of horizontal accountability and the role of society and the electorate in vertical accountability, deconstructing accountability requires an analysis of the state, how the state interacts with society, and what this means for understanding accountability.

First, we examine the construct of the state. We follow this with an analysis of the relationship between state and society; then introduce the role of the citizen by considering what is meant by 'civil society'. This discussion is located within a recent move in the literature to debate how society and the state sit together (Hobson 2001). We look particularly at elites, who link the state and society and wield the greatest power. The concept of the state depends on which school of thought is followed and, indeed, which discipline the analysis rests on. We apply a broadly political economy definition of the state here, focusing on issues of power distribution.

## The State

The state is a concept that is central to many disciplines, yet it remains a widely debated term. The state has spread as a standard form of organisation throughout the world. From the functionalist perspective, states do not exist by virtue of their effectiveness, but rather because they are supported by a 'larger world culture' (Finnemore 1996: 332). It is necessary to be organised within a state to participate in global politics. The boundaries of state organisation show a high degree of stability: even as regimes are challenged and changed the state as a unit persists, dominating alternative forms of organisation, such as the economic, the ethnic and the religious, which may take the form of empires, colonies and fiefdoms (Meyer 1987).

How does this book understand the state? We apply an analytical Marxist framework, as this incorporates political conflict theory with a specific focus on elite confrontations (for discussion on the latter see below). We use Gramsci's broad view of the state based on his notion of power by consent, which is linked to Lucas' latent or ideological power. Within this, we draw on the concept of the shadow state. This places hegemony and the use of ideology at the core of the state. As the shadow state is usually applied to countries in chaos and conflict, and used to analyse the role of violence, we follow Reno's view that the shadow state is a 'matter of degree' (2000: 442), and draw out salient elements such as patronage and informal connections, networks and elites. Corruption is the efficient operation of predation. Given it is systemic and deliberate, corruption is therefore normalised, rather than involving a breaking of norms. The exercise of power is based on the threat of violence and a subsequent need to maintain stability, operating through ideology.

Weber saw the state as broader than mere government; and as the organisation that controls territories, as well as the people that inhabit those territories, which holds the monopoly on the legitimate use of physical force. The state is organised around administrative, legal, extractive and coercive organisations, which structure relations both within society, as well as between society and the state (Skocpol 1985), and are embedded within a constitutional and representative parliamentary structure (Weber 1919, 1991). Within the state there are therefore different units and forms of authority, as public sector agencies are involved in governance, coordinated by the executive, and have the authority and capacity to implement binding rules (Routley 2012).

In this Weberian definition, authority (which places us within reach of accountability) is strongly hierarchical, such that direct responsibility for the actions of a particular ministry rest with the appointed minister and a narrow view of ministerial responsibility is upheld, exemplified by frequent political resignations in response to accusations. 'The honour of the political leader ... lies precisely in an exclusive personal responsibility for what he does, a responsibility that he cannot and must not reject or transfer' (Weber 1919, 1991: 95). This hierarchical structure has roots that are found throughout the works of Weber and points to a separation of the political leadership, supported by an executive administration (Bovens 1998: 75).

However, the reality of states may differ from the Weberian ideal type. While the state is often considered to be a homogeneous entity, it does in fact consist of different agencies which may pull in different directions. Therefore, within the state there are issues of power relations and bargaining which limit the power states have to make rules (Migdal 1988). Migdal (1988) defines four state capabilities: the ability to penetrate society; to regulate social relations; to extract resources; and to use these resources. These are interdependent – the capability of the state to regulate social relations and to extract resources has an impact on its ability to penetrate society and the use to which it puts those resources. Gramsci (1971) saw this relationship clearly and described the state as the 'entire complex of practical and theoretical activities with which the ruling class not only justifies and maintains its dominance, but manages to win the active consent of those over whom it rules'.

The shadow state can be illustrated by contrasting it to the Hobbesian state. The Hobbesian state exists as an artificial monster and has control of the monopoly of force to ensure the protection of its members. In this way, it ensures an outcome that is orderly and in stark contrast to the disorder that would naturally arise through 'the state of nature', when the state is absent (Hobbes 1651, 1909). In contrast, the legitimacy of the shadow state is still underpinned by the social contract, but instead of ensuring the protection of the population it creates insecurity to enhance the power of the leadership. It is based on an individual and personal rule constructed behind a façade of official institutions which include formal, written legislation. It undermines these institutions through its ability to manipulate access to markets so as to maximise the power of the incumbent (Reno 2000). Patronage is used as a means of political control by limiting the provision of public goods (including security and economic stability) and thus ensuring reliance on informal networks and connections. The leader encourages dependence on personal favour and cultivates insecurity, instability and, in some cases, even violence; therefore, legitimacy is neither sought nor necessary. If the leader secures a monopoly over power, however, the resulting legitimacy may allow investment in the productive capacity of the ruled, and enable a movement from a situation of net welfare loss and instability to a net welfare gain and stability, as corruption is institutionalised (Reno 2000). The resulting extensive dependence on patronage, operating through networks overseen by a personalised leadership, is part of the nature of the shadow state. A characteristic of the shadow state is the personalised and private nature of the relationships between elites and the leadership (Reno 2000) and the blurring of the private and public spheres (Kelsall 2002).

The state cannot, of course, exist independently. Therefore, before considering the relationship between the state and society, we must first turn to look at society itself. Examining the term 'society' and its compatriot 'civil society', leads towards a discussion of elites and the positioning of society in relation to the state.

## Society

As the concept of accountability has, since the 1990s, gained popularity in development, there has been a focus on increased transparency and on strengthening the capacity of civil society to demand increased accountability from the state.

Civil society becomes relevant as citizens move towards collective groups based on shared identities and common roles. It commonly falls into the realm of procedural accountability and it is grounded in the concepts of voice and political freedom, exemplified in the work of Hirschman (1970) and Sen (1999), that draw on the notion of political freedom and assume that the more open and inclusive the dialogue, the greater is its ability to sanction public performance. The instrumental value of political freedom is expressed through accountability channels such as voting, courts and the space for a free press. Voice also plays a constructive role through the increase in deliberation and open debate among groups in consideration of social goals and their associated trade-offs. The realities of clientelism and the complexities of relational accountability present an immediate challenge to achieving this. In Chapter 2 we stressed the plurality of different identities and the dynamic nature of social relations. We also discussed the heterogeneity of civil society organisations and their democratic limitations due to inequalities of power, lack of internal democratic process and accountability to members and the risk of co-optation by funders (Jelmin 2012, Rocha Menocal and Sharma 2008). We explore these aspects further by considering the collective identity of civil society, to allow us to then consider civil society in relation to the state.

Reno (2000) sees the relationship between the state and society as one whereby the ruler attempts to undermine any efforts towards collective organisation to ensure that dependence on the bestowing of favours is maintained. Funke and Solomon (2002) argue that, ideally, an effective civil society should be independent of the state and not created by it, although they acknowledge that political groups may evolve from the state. These perspectives note the challenges in establishing an effective civil society and the reality that its capacity and independence are limited.

Most commonly in the literature, the term 'civil society' refers to the coming together of groups that are able to organise themselves politically. While civil society is commonly understood to refer to formal organisations, should it be limited to officially recognised bodies or be as broad as to include clientelistic networks (Chabal and Daloz 1999)? Civil society can, of course, start as an informal network sharing common interests and may only recognise themselves as civil society when they become aware of their ability to organise and to influence. For example in Iran Foucault noted a self-consciousness to the existence of civil society and an explicit opposition to the state in the 'collective will' of a people in Iran, whereby civil society was aware of its own existence and positioning (Kritzman and Foucault 1990, 1988: 218). African organisations are naturally typified by 'cultural, religious, linguistic rifts' (Bayart 1986: 117) that lend themselves to collective wills, even if they are not entirely self-conscious. The term 'civil society' emphasises this uncomfortable juxtaposition of the state against society and, while Chabal and Daloz (1999: 19) question what the addition of the term 'civil' brings, here we use it to emphasise the collective. In the strongest use of the term, it invokes recognition of a collective identity by the actors within the groups and by others outside the groups. In moving towards considering the relationship between the state and society, we now discuss national elites.

*Elites, the State and Society*

Elites are central to this analysis, as conceptually they allow us to build in conflict between competing groups. Conceptualising the elite brings together the structural (macro), the institutionalist (meso) and the agent (micro) by presenting an analytical interface between society and the state. We consolidate an interface between the actor, the role of norms and the place of these within the social structure. From this we consider dependency and power relations.

Lachmann defines elites 'by their control over organisational apparatuses for appropriating resources from non-elites ... constrained primarily by coexisting elites' (1990: 398). Elites as a tool in historical analysis were first examined by Mosca and Pareto (1896, 1901 cited in Lachmann 1990: 398, 400), who considered them to exist only temporarily and to be challenged or to decay in the longer run. C. Wright Mills (1956, 2000) allowed for the permanence of elites by combining structural and institutional factors with the social and the personal, extending earlier analyses and drawing on Weber's bureaucratic authority. Analysing structure of power in the United States during the Cold War, he noted that structural changes in power had resulted from shifts in the 'relative positions of the political, the economic and the military orders' (Mills 1956, 2000: 269). Such changes resulted in specific characteristics such as stronger links between business and government, growth of the executive branch and an enlarged role for the military (Mills 1956, 2000). He saw these structural characteristics as being underpinned by personal and official relations, and accorded the role of the actor a significance that involved the '[c]o-optation of the social types to which [these] common values lead' as arising through social discipline and a community of interests (Mills 1956, 2000: 281–283). This is not to imply that he recognised only consensus and cohesion; rather, he acknowledged factions whereby conflicts of policy and individual ambitions operated alongside discipline and co-optation. Another key characteristic that Mills observed was the fluidity of elites, and that the 'nature of the power elite is that within it there is a good deal of shifting about' (Mills 1956, 2000: 287). This results from the combination of personal friendships with active co-optation, invoking relational characteristics.

More recent work concurs with the notion that elites are made up of powerful decision makers: a small number of people controlling the 'key material, symbolic and political resources', occupying 'commanding' positions within key institutions (Reis and Moore 2005: 2) or those with the power and influence to 'determine which policies are implemented, when and how as well as the rules of the game' (Kalebe-Nyamongo 2009: 2). Elites, in a national context, comprise those

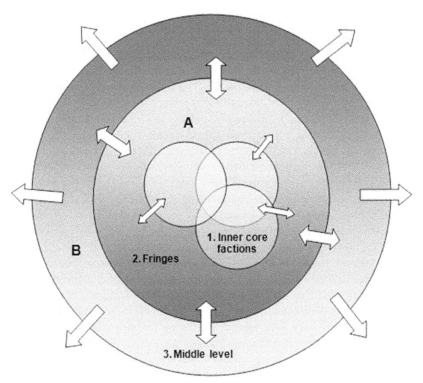

**Figure 3.1    The structure of elites in society**

*Source:* Author's interpretation of C. Wright Mills (1956, 2000).

occupying the top positions in a country's institutions: the political institutions of the legislature, presidency, cabinet and political parties; the civil service; the police and armed forces; large companies and business organisations; large landowners; trade unions; the media; educational and professional organisations; voluntary associations; and religious institutions (Reis and Moore 2005, Dogan 2003). These different affiliations of members of elites cuts across the different tiers of elites (shown in Figure 3.1), and it is the different levels that will be focussed on here. 'State class' is a useful term, as it covers members of the political, administrative and economic elites, which we can place in relation to the different tiers.

Mills identified three tiers of elites: 1) the inner core; 2) the outermost fringes; and 3) the tier below the fringes, or the middle level of power. The inner core is made up of the decision makers, who rotate between commanding roles at the top of organisations. The outermost fringes contain 'those who count' and who are taken into decisive account when decisions are being made, even if they are not personally present (Mills 1956, 2000: 290). This tier is more fluid than the core. Finally, the middle level of power consists of pressure groups that are not vested in the elite: regional, state and local interests and the rank and file who must sometimes be taken into account, handled, cajoled and raised into the higher circles, if support is needed to achieve a specific end (Mills 1956, 2000). We simplify these three tiers into two levels: A) the interior – the inner core and the fringes, contesting power at the top levels of society, and where the state class is located; and B) the exterior – the middle level of power, providing the interrelationship between elites and the rest of society and support to those in power through patron–client networks (Figure 3.1). The arrows in Figure 3.1 illustrate the direction of influence between the three tiers. For instance between the inner core factions and the fringes within Level A, the interior; and also between Levels A and B, there is a two way influence as relationships exist and influence is exerted. In contrast there is only a one way, and downward influence between Level B and the rest of society. This is because those in Level B, the exterior, are not influenced by those who are marginalised and neither exercise voice nor have resources, such as power, to exert influence.

We can aid the analysis of the contestation between elites by invoking the notion of factions supported by an informal network. We do not consider elites to be homogeneous and consensual. Rather they are heterogeneous, built around conflict and differing interests that compete with one another. This reflects the dynamism within society that is a continual test of the legitimisation of ruling elites, and captures the different interests described by Reis and Moore (2005) and Dogan (2003). These elite networks can cut across formal and informal interests or organisations ranging from state institutions such as the civil service, political parties and parliament; to non-governmental and civil society organisations; to the private sector. Many individual actors are influential within more than one of these categories. Particularly strong networks may result in different factions forming coalitions, which may be formal or informal, temporary or permanent (Leftwich 2010). Chabal and Daloz (1999) consider the connections between 'high' and 'low' politics, or political elites and their clientelistic networks. They see these relationships as central in determining the mechanisms of power and social control. Developing a 'circle of trust' through a large support network is particularly important in the absence of an autonomous and impartial state (Chabal et al. 1999: 27). The strength of these networks relative to the strength of the leadership determines the degree of centralisation of power and rent seeking. That is, the leadership's ability to directly centralise power depends on the relative strength of the competing factions.

While there has been some debate around the proportion of society that is considered to be elite (Leftwich 2010, Dahl 1958, 1968), perhaps a more important question is how to determine why an actor is included in an elite. An individual can be included if they meet two criteria: 1) they are central to the operation of an elite faction; and 2) they have the ability to leave and create a rival elite faction (Lachmann 1990). The risk of an actor's departure resulting in the creation of a rival elite faction is an example of co-optation through elite networks, which is an important result of the process of contestation through which power is exercised.

What role do elite confrontations and conflict play in social change or stability? The specific nature of elites is of course a direct function of the political economy of each country. A common thread in the literature is that elite support is necessary for the maintenance of political power (Lindemann and Putzel 2008, North et al. 2007). Elites can also be seen as the manifestation of political power which is maintained through ideology. Particularly when viewed through the lens of latent power, ideology – or the dominant paradigm – is transmitted through language and other forms of communication. The more effective its domination, the less likely is elite conflict. Applying the concept of the shadow state, elites dominate through groups that serve well-established interests, and the elite bargain is the outcome that provides the winning coalition with incentives to be peaceful by limiting access to rents to those within the coalition (North et al. 2007). Given this incentive to maintain both power and in turn minimise confrontations, Lachmann (2000) concludes that elite conflict rarely achieves the intended results, however he argues that '[it] is the bright thread of agency that propelled structural changes in all situations'.

This brings us to the question of legitimisation. How do elites maintain support from the rest of society? In other words, how are they legitimated? Furthermore, to what extent does their legitimisation explain why some ideas and practices are institutionalised and others are not? Gramsci (1971) claims that elite domination of the consciousness of members of other classes explains the institutionalisation of ideas and practices. Taking this into account, the question then becomes, how is such domination maintained? Ruling elites maintain support through patronage payments, underwritten by the latent operation of power such that the system of support becomes institutionalised and accepted: this is the main interface between the two levels, A and B in Figure 3.1. These payments to obtain the support of the rest of society require a coalition between political and business elites, as linkages between politics and business are used to identify opportunities and siphon off rents to allow redistribution to a wider group. This 'requires off-budget 'redistribution' through patron–client networks to achieve political stabilization. The corrupt exchange here involves politicians … transferring resources to powerful clients and receiving, in exchange, their political support' (Khan 2004b: 14).

*Political party elites*
A political party is itself an elite or a coalition of elites. It is firmly part of an interface with society, as it is influenced by and influences society. In this sense, the party and the leadership are influenced by the societal structures of power and legitimacy, which are dominated by different elites and their networks. As we will see below, elites must also be conceptually placed within the agency-structure interface as, although the notion of leadership is distanced from that of individual personalities, elites are composed of actors who are at once constrained by, but yet also able to influence, the structure of society.

Can a change in political regime or institutions be accompanied by a compensatory change in power relationships such that elite power persists? The interests of powerful elites can be sustained in a democracy, as there is rarely a complete circulation of elites or a wholesale shift in power to different groups (other than in the event of a coup). Elites are pervasive as a result of their flexibility and capacity to adapt (Chabal and Daloz 1999). De facto political power (determined by the equilibrium investments of different groups, based on wealth or collective action) can compensate for a loss in de jure power (allocations determined by political institutions) (Acemoglu and Robinson 2007).

In democracy, de jure power favours the electorate; whereas elites in a non-democracy have greater de jure power. Acemoglu and Robinson (2007) argue that, in a democracy, elites respond to incentives by investing in de facto power to compensate for reduced de jure power. Drawing on Mosca (1939) and Olson (1965) they find that the elite are more likely than the non-elite to invest in de facto power in a democracy as they are smaller in number than the electorate and can expect greater returns from controlling politics. They find that elite domination is lower when the gains from controlling institutions are reduced through, for example, more competitive economic institutions. Moreover, increased democracy creates an increased future cost for elites; they therefore aim to increase their de facto power to offset this expected higher future cost. The authors note that democracy may therefore not be advantageous for the electorate, as economic institutions favour elites, terming this outcome a 'captured democracy' (Acemoglu and Robinson 2007: 3).

Why do many democracies pursue pro-elite policies? And why do inefficient states persist? Answering these questions helps us understand the form of accountability that might arise in a democracy. An inefficient state structure can create more rents for bureaucrats, and elites can therefore use patronage and capture democratic politics (Acemoglu et al. 2007). These rents may in turn support the party that will maintain the inefficient structure and, by extension, an inefficient state is more likely to arise when there is greater income and wealth inequality.

There is, however, no justification for the assumption that elite economic institutions will be less efficient than those preferred by other actors in society. In reality preferences are not rational, as we discuss below. The demarcation between actors and elites are, nevertheless, not always clear and formalised. Rather, there is often a complex and informal system of networks and allegiances, making it difficult to clearly identify the two groups, as described in Figure 3.1

*International elites*
Moving beyond the nation state to the international, defined as 'transnational forces, processes and institutions not based on the state' (Sklair 2001: 2), is important for our analysis of aid relations. Robinson (2010: 7) notes the structural distinction between the national elites, who are linked to the protected state industries and working classes, and the transnational elites, who are routed in 'globalized circuits of accumulation' and look to global markets.

This transnational class (also termed the 'global ruling class' or the 'global elite') is the meeting of progressive groups of national elites from the North and South on the stage of international development and based on a common middle-class. This meeting arises through the commonality of class and interests arising from increased globalisation and operates within the Washington Consensus or neoliberal agenda (Robinson and Harris 2000). It is important to distinguish between international organisations such as the World Bank and the International Monetary Fund, and transnational organisations, such as advocacy movements and some multinational businesses: the former are accountable to nation states, whereas the transnational transcends both states and nations.

The discussion of the transnational usually focuses on private sector corporations, through the internationalisation of capital. However, here we extend the concept to public sector international development organisations (such as bilateral donors) to illustrate how national elites create an effective interface with international development actors. In doing so, elites can communicate through the use of the same concepts and by sharing a common language of poverty reduction and aid delivery. 'World ruling class formation is seen as the international collusion of these national bourgeoisies and their resultant international coalitions' (Robinson and Harris 2000: 3). The operation of networks can be seen through the overseas schools that elites in developing countries send their children to, as well as the location of second residencies and university networks in Europe and America. The persistence of factionalism is noted within the transnational elite:

Fierce competition among oligopolistic clusters, conflicting pressures, and differences over the tactics and strategy of maintaining class domination and addressing the crises and contradictions of global capitalism make any real internal unity in the global ruling class impossible (Robinson and Harris 2000).

*Summarising elites*
The working definition of elites that we apply here follows the visual representation in Figure 3.1. It is based on Mills' (1956, 2000) interplay of the institutional and structural with the personal and social. Groups, or factions, within elites are characterised by consensus and cohesion through co-optation and common values. Added to this is a continual contestation between the factions in the inner core of elites, resulting in fluidity as actors move between factions and between positions. These factions function within a network and, where the network strongly represents common interests, coalitions may form. The implicit influence of power in shaping perceptions and views is important for understanding how elites reproduce their ideology and co-opt others into their networks.

As elites use patronage to capture democratic politics, and the party is supported by the rents (Acemoglu et al. 2007), this is linked to inequality and lower levels of economic competitiveness whereby an inefficient state structure creates rents for bureaucrats. While here we focus on national elites, in Chapter 5 we consider how elites may extend beyond the national, depending on the nature of national politics. This extension may include transnational elites that operate at regional and global levels (Robinson and Harris 2000).

What does this conceptualisation of elites imply for accountability? Elites and their role in society do not fit well with the traditional procedural notion of accountability, which provides neither space for the differential power of the tiers nor for the factions within the inner core (see Figure 3.1). In contrast, procedural and traditional accountability is based on the implicit assumption of equality across actors; society is simply an aggregation of individual preferences and therefore a homogenous black box. The reality is that elites evoke the personal through the notions of culture, influence and co-optation, and depend on an interface between agency and structure. This is important for facilitating a common understanding beyond the national level, within the international development circle, operating through informal elite networks.

*The State within Society*

The concept of elites is central to an analysis of the relationship between the state and society, as it permeates both, facilitating consideration of the interaction between the two and, in turn, the mechanisms through which power is contested. Since the work of Hobbes and Locke, some literature has retained a distinction between the state and society in contrast to this emphasis of their interrelationship (Migdal 1988).

Influenced by Gramsci (1971), Chabal and Daloz (1999), Gupta (1995) and Migdal (2001), we consider the state and society to be integrated, and societal institutions to be the ideological apparatus of the state from which they cannot be separated. Gramsci (1971) notes that, in certain states, the head of state is also the head of the political party, maintaining the balance of power within civil society through its hegemonic function and influence across different groups. This presents a view of the state, or 'political society', as intertwined with civil society and thus both ruling and governing. Gramsci draws on Hegel's conception of the parties and associations of society as the 'private woof of the state', such that the state is governed with consent through hegemony, protected by the armour of coercion, and stresses that the state reaches beyond government to the 'private apparatus of ... civil society' (Gramsci 1971: 259, 261, 263). This consent is related to the discussion above of the coalition of elites, as the state manufactures such consent by actively encouraging and co-opting private elites.

The degree of engagement or disengagement of the state puts boundaries on the extent to which it can penetrate society, and therefore regulate social relations. This may owe to resistance, mutual disengagement, aspects of society that are beyond the influence of the state – or a combination of these. The state is a mélange that exists within society where heterogeneous and autonomous groups have control (Migdal 2001). This limits the extent of control of the state, as control can be distributed among a number of groups, which may themselves be in conflict with one another. Examples of such groups include the church, ethnic groups, villages and language groups (Migdal 1988). Such a 'web-like' model of society fits with observations of African societies, as identified by Iliffe (1971) and Kelsall (2004). This shares some similarities with the model used by Chandhoke (2003), who describes the state as being represented by many agencies and organisations and sharing power with sub-national and partnership organisations including international agencies.

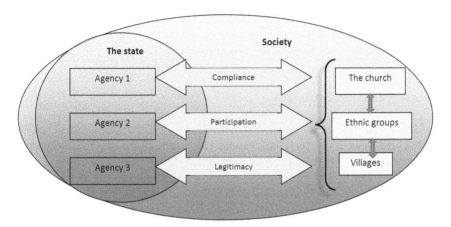

**Figure 3.2 The state in society**

*Source:* Author's representation of Migdal (1988, 2001).

Social control is based on compliance, participation and legitimacy (Migdal 1988), and we might view the relationship between state and society as being based on these three functions, as Figure 3.2 illustrates. Here, the three functions are presented as a tension between state and society, with the state placed within society. Compliance is achieved by the perpetuation of the dominant ideology of the elite; where this fails, agencies (such as the police) are used to obtain compliance to the rules of the state. Participation here is not of the type typically denoted in poverty reduction strategy papers, which refer to citizen voice, but refers to the voluntary use of state institutions, which increases the strength of the state as actors are organised to participate in them. Such organisation encompasses, for example, the need to obtain licences as well as the cooperative structures for selling agricultural produce. Legitimation can be seen as the successful outcome of bargaining for power, as compliance and participation have been achieved and the role and authority of the state have been accepted and have the approval of the people. In short, the greater the extent of compliance, participation and legitimacy, the greater the control of the state.

This theory cannot fully explain the mechanism through which legitimacy is created and sustained. Nor does it give sufficient emphasis to the role of elites and conflict. Therefore, it is supplemented by the shadow state and the elite. The individual and personal rule of the shadow state relies on patronage, informal connections, networks and the elite. In the shadow state, corruption is necessary for predation to operate efficiently, and it is therefore normalised, although not necessarily explicitly. Patronage is a key mechanism through which power is exercised and insecurity is created to ensure a reliance on the distribution of rents, which, in turn, are used to restore an element of stability such that the incumbent retains power (Reno 2000). Bringing in elites allows for the interplay of the institutional and structural with the personal and social, and consensus and cohesion are induced through co-optation. Continual contestation among the factions within the inner core of elites functions through a network of connections as actors move between factions and between positions.

## 3.4 Accountability and Society

The deconstruction of procedural-accountability in this chapter centres on its location within the lower levels of Williamson's hierarchy. A fundamental weakness is the lack of acknowledgement in international development of the higher-level factors that frame the range of possible outcomes. This can also explain why some reforms are successful and others fail. It is through considering Level 1 influences that we can understand the concept of relational accountability and its interaction with procedural accountability located in the lower levels. The sections that follow explore this analysis of the concepts that underlie procedural accountability, concluding with a proposal for a new understanding of accountability.

*Rationality*

Rationality is an important assumption that underpins procedural accountability, yet pure rationality ignores the influence of social norms on decisions. The recognition of cognitive limitations, on the other hand, recognises a psychological basis to decision making and as influencing social norms. This takes us into the realm of relational accountability. Behaviour results from individual deliberation and captures social norms from the experiences and the programmable nature of the human mind (Ostrom 1998, Simon 1973).

Bounded rationality introduces constraints on the information-processing capacities of the actor and turns its focus to the agent and the importance of 'our view of the nature of the human beings whose behaviour we are studying' (Simon 1985: 303). The location of these bounds on rationality within methodological individualism remains too restrictive. In orthodox economics, bounded rationality has become implicitly adopted as an objectively specified standard of behaviour, and is supported by methodological individualism, which becomes problematic when it is extended to take account of higher-level social influences and constraints. This mirrors the constraints of procedural accountability. It is bounded rationality that moves towards the assumptions of rationality that are found also in sociology, psychology and history.

Within sociology, rationality is most commonly referred to as a process whereby a collective social purpose is achieved through social organisation that is a result of the 'structuring of everyday life within standardised impersonal rules' (Meyer et al. 1987: 24). This rationalisation of society results in a movement towards a collective pursuit of progress and justice, originating from Western society and now adopted as a global goal. Perhaps the largest body of literature on different types of rationality that underlies this process has Weberian roots.

Weber identified the movement towards an increasingly rational–legal system of authority and away from traditional and charismatic forms, resulting from a process of rationalisation in pursuit of efficiency (Cockerham et al. 1993, Kalberg 1980). The type of rationality that underpins procedural accountability is analogous to Weber's notion of formal rationality, which he recognises as emerging in the West alongside industrialisation. Formal rationality involves a means-end calculation, with the focus on efficiency in the context of universal laws. He focused on the interplay between formal and substantive rationality, whereby substantive rationality relates to the system of values (Cockerham et al. 1993), characteristics of which are displayed within relational accountability.

Within sociology and social psychology, writers including Bourdieu and Nadel offer different understandings of the existence and emergence of rationality, leading to questions about the assumptions made about agency and actor motivations and how and why standards of behaviour become legitimised as international norms. They reject the notion that actors act purposively, considering behaviour to frequently be an automatic response to social norms (Bourdieu, 1990, Nadel, 1957 cited in MacDonald 2003: 556). This leads to an argument for extending the preference function to include elements such as conformity with social norms, involving a movement away from methodological individualism as a theoretical basis towards considering individuals as members of social groups, and an upward movement from Level 4 to higher-levels of Williamson's social hierarchy (Williamson 2000).

Globalisation has seen the spread of the Western culture of capitalism to the extent that it has become an international hegemony. The characteristics that have accompanied the spread of market capitalism include individualism, marketisation and varying degrees of liberalism. Rationalism is a core value on which individual action is based, whereby action is structured in terms of ends and means. This motivation is assumed to override other ways in which social action could be structured, including through rituals, obligations, roles and duties (Finnemore 1996). Some branches of international relations have recognised the limitations of the rationality assumption, given the persistence of organisations that are inefficient. Furthermore, aspects of the sociological theory of structuration – whereby 'institutions constitute actors as well as constrain them and interests emerge within particular normative and historical contexts' (DiMaggio and Powell 1991: 7) – has been applied to international relations theories.

While traditional and new institutionalism places the individual within an institution, it continues to emphasise the rational and the convergence towards one global system through a focus on governance structures and formal rules. A comparative institutionalism has emerged that reopens the tension between structure and agency and brings about a renewed focus on culture (Drori 2008). Applying Williamson's hierarchy, heterodox branches of economics, sociology and social psychology move up towards higher-levels that allow consideration of the social structure and both the formal and the informal rules that frame and constrain behaviour and economic and social outcomes. We now examine this through a discussion of agency, motivation and structure, followed by an analysis of their relevance for the concepts of procedural accountability and relational accountability.

## Agency, Motivation and Structure

Procedural-accountability has a specific and narrow context that considers only immediate events. It is separated from the wider social system and starts from the basis that agency is independent of structure, in line with the spread of individualism through globalisation. However, the interaction of agency and structure in determining behaviour points to the need for accountability to be considered through a broader lens. What capacity do individuals have to act independently (agency) and how do social rules (structure) influence their behaviour?

### Agency and motivation

Older sociological and anthropological theories saw action as a result of the enactment of rules and norms (Ortner 1984). The rise of the investigation into the concept of agency in the social sciences can be traced to the 1970s, with writers from Bourdieu in anthropology (1977) to Giddens in sociology (1979) to Thompson in history (1978) calling for an increased focus on the subject or the agent (Ortner 1984). While this appears to be moving in the direction of methodological individualism, and therefore towards procedural accountability, it does not go to the extreme of total freedom without constraints; rather, it explicitly allows for a greater influence of cognition, calculation, strategising and active choice. The recognition of a greater role for action, agency and motivation permits a greater range of responses to situations, although such agency is a relative concept. Agency is determined by the capacity of actors to act independently of constraints that may exist in the form of social norms (Gulrajani 2010). The extent to which constraints may influence behaviour, through the interaction of agency with structure, determines the boundaries of procedural accountability.

Motivation as 'the organisation of an actor's wants' implies conscious and unconscious emotions and cognition (Giddens 1979: 58). Inasmuch as the unconscious is involved, unintended consequences of action may result, which are central to the reproduction of institutions. The needs or wants of actors are therefore independent of the social, political and cultural context (Finnemore 1996).

While the operation of accountability is based on the existence of such tensions and the differing motivations of different groups and individuals, this remains implicit in procedural accountability. Procedural accountability is based on methodological individualism, where the individual is the key unit of analysis and organisations are simply the sum of individual preference functions. The structure of the collective group has no influence on behaviour and state agencies of horizontal accountability are black boxes. It addresses neither the fundamental motivations that underlie such actions nor the unintended consequences that result from unconscious motivations. These omissions crucially overlook an examination of the role of agency or action. This individualism is challenged by studies on structure, as well as studies on the interaction between structure and action, the latter which determine the extent of agency.

*Structure*

The concept of structure is central to the work of a number of sociologists (including Marx, Parsons and Giddens) and appears in the writings of many more. Structure refers to the pattern of social relations and is related to the function, or how such patterns of social relations operate as social systems (in the theory of functionalism). According to the theory of structuralism, it also refers to social transformations through its operation at deep sub-structure levels. Deep structures are pervasive and often taken for granted. They operate across a range of settings and generate a range of surface structures. Regardless of the power it embodies, a deep structure is durable in comparison to the more dynamic surface structure. This distinction is analogous to the differing pervasiveness and depth of Williamson's levels. To illustrate this, Sewell (1992) takes the example of a state structure, where a high degree of power and a lack of depth result in a high probability that contestation will take place as its lack of durability is recognised.

Placing actors' behaviour and decisions in the context of a structure removes the overly energetic pursuit of goals and continual rational calculations they would otherwise have to undertake. This is not to imply they become passive, as there is a two-way interaction between agency and structure, but rather the interaction between norms and action removes the excessive rationality of actors, a criticism that has resulted in the charge of 'too much active-ness' (Ortner 1984: 151). There is a reflexive component of action whereby an agent monitors his or her action and provides reasons, or rationalisations, for it. This takes place firmly within the social setting. Giddens claims rationalisation is more complex than simply an assessment of behaviour with reference to norms, rectifying the earlier discussion on the omission of cognition (Giddens 1979, DiMaggio and Powell 1991). While agency as presented by Giddens and cultural anthropologists is based on actors' knowledge of rules; the content of such knowledge is omitted (Sewell 1992: 7).

Social rules are applied reflexively, thus allowing for outcomes that may include integrity and altruism and therefore may diverge from the pure rationalist outcome (Giddens 1979, 1984). Rules include conventions, scenarios, habits and principles; in other words, cultural schemas that can be informal as well as formal. Such schemas can be generalised beyond their original usage and operate at a range of depths: from within deep structures to the superficial.

Individuals' motivation might extend beyond self-interest to include reflection and morality. Such morality is not impotent, but results from the depth of socialisation and the internalisation of norms that are maintained through sanctions, rather than the sanctions directly influencing the behaviour of the majority (Bovens 1998). The government plays an active role in perpetuating such norms through campaigns and propaganda. Dwivedi and Jabbra (1988) highlight that traditional (procedural) accountability omits morals and their impact on behaviour.

What does the interaction between agency and structure mean for the theory of accountability? The influence of social rules on the behaviour of individuals removes the capacity for purely independent and behaviour that is not influenced by social norms. Placing this within Williamson's hierarchy, it clearly points towards factors within Level 1 constraining and influencing the outcomes that arise within the lower levels. As procedural accountability focuses on assumptions arising from the lower levels, it is clear that there are key elements are influential and that procedural-accountability cannot take adequate account of.

## 3.5 Summary: Accountability Deconstructed

This chapter has deconstructed what is meant by accountability through an examination of its underlying epistemological assumptions. We have examined the concepts of power; rationality; agency and structure; culture and legitimacy, and critiqued them from an interdisciplinary perspective. By going beyond the individualistic and rationalistic methodology of orthodox economics, and applying the work of sociologists, anthropologists, psychologists and philosophers, we have drawn out the limitations of the procedural notion of accountability.

Procedural accountability is a concept that emerges directly from Western culture and is implicitly based on an epistemology whereby actors – either principals or agents – are rational utility maximisers, transactions are impersonal, rules are formal and contractual in nature, and the pursuit of self-interest is assumed to lead to moral hazard in the absence of full information. The accountability contract arises when a principal exercises authority over an agent's actions, the authority being embodied in a judgement of whether responsibilities have been met, assessed against objective and externally specified standards (Grant and Keohane 2005). Thus, accountability in the 'hard' form fills the role of enforcing appropriate behaviour, with the threat of sanction necessary to enforce the appropriate behaviour (Fox 2007, Schedler 1999). This stems from the assumption that, in the absence of a threat of sanction, the pursuit of self-interest would lead to the misappropriation of resources.

Analyses of the assumptions that underpin the procedural notion of accountability suggest it has only limited application in reality – unsurprising given their simplification. For rationality, what matters is not whether the behaviour of individuals or institutions are rational or not, but what is meant by rationality. In other words, what is included in the preference function? And to what extent does bounded rationality capture the necessarily elements? If we include concepts drawn from sociology and cultural anthropology, such as culture, social structure and ideological power, we can form a broader perspective of accountability that includes elements that are informal and appear to be inconsistent and irrational if we are restricted to the narrower preference function. The result of this broadening of the preference function is that it is no longer sufficiently simple to be testable. It becomes complex, iterative, recursive and dynamic – characteristics that are found in reality.

Agency and structure interact closely. A greater role for action, agency and motivation permits a greater range of responses to stimuli, and this demands an alternative model of accountability and has important implications for aid policy (Leftwich and Wheeler 2011). Moreover, the interaction between norms and action removes the simplicity of the rationality of actors embodied within procedural accountability. Agency is therefore a relative concept, determined by the capacity of actors to act independently of constraints that may exist in the form of social norms (Gulrajani 2010). This implies a reflexive component of action whereby an agent monitors their own action and provides reasons for such action, or rationalises their action; and this reflexivity occurs within the social setting.

A weakness in the traditional rationalist and procedural understanding of accountability is the lack of a comprehensive analysis of the highly context-specific and complex cultural factors that underlie the relationships around which accountability is formed. These factors are based on interpersonal relationships between actors and are a function of the specific social context, capturing the interplay between actors and social institutions. When the procedural accountability model alone is applied these factors are overlooked: behaviour cannot be fully explained and conflict may arise. The relational understanding of accountability overcomes this by capturing the complex interrelationships between institutions at the local level and the interplay of the different currents influencing accountability, including religion, socialism, the cash economy and democracy (Kelsall et al. 2005).

This dissimilarity is rooted in the different epistemological roots of procedural-accountability and relational accountability. Procedural accountability is founded in orthodox economics and draws on rational public choice models, serving a functional need to achieve the rationalist standards of 'effectiveness, efficiency, lawfulness or greater productivity' (Gulrajani 2010: 8). Relational accountability allows for the influence of social norms and a psychological basis to decision making. Relational accountability is therefore complex, highly personalised, underpinned by implicit and informal rules, and a function of specific and dynamic political and social relations.

This discussion has pointed to a more complex underpinning to what accountability may mean and the limitations of restricting understanding to the procedural form of accountability, highlighted by a number of writers (Bovens 1998, Ebrahim 2009, Eyben 2007, Gulrajani 2010). What emerges from this analysis is the need for an additional form of accountability; one that considers complex, highly personalised, and often contradictory, political and social relations based on implicit, informal and accidental rules. This broader and more culturally relevant understanding of accountability is termed 'relational accountability' and is located within the highest tier of Williamson's framework (see Figure 1.3).

Relational accountability has emerged from this multidisciplinary understanding of culture; the interface between agency and structure; the critique of rationality; and the positioning of the state in society and the role of elites and power. Elites are at the core of the analysis, given the pivotal role they play in influencing policies and decisions, and linking the state and society. The reach of accountability stretches out in a web-like structure, capturing actors as they function within a multitude of different social roles within elite networks. Relational accountability depends on the process of power at play in all relations, and is subtly demonstrated through language. This type of accountability allows for an analysis of the role of obligations and patronage in a reciprocal relationship that is influenced by social norms, culture and power.

The nature of power differs in the two typographies. Through the procedural accountability lens, it is a contractual resource that is limited and rests with either the principal or the agent. In contrast, through the relational accountability lens, power is a fluid capacity that latently underpins all interactions and is unlimited. Power is enacted through clientelistic networks: covertly through the shaping of perceptions and explicitly when the more powerful clients impose constraints on the state. This influence depends on blurred boundaries between the public and private and on an informalisation, where formal rules are not seen as important (Chabal and Daloz 1999, Bratton and Van de Walle 1997, Jackson and Rosberg 1982, Médard 1982).

Finally, and resulting from these characteristics, the mode of behaviour of procedural accountability is rational and measurable. When viewed from the perspective of procedural accountability, the behaviour arising from relational concerns appears to be irrational, as it responds to wider social norms and longer-term accountability relations. This makes it problematic to measure.

We now apply this theory to enable an understanding of how current aid policy has failed. In the next chapter we will look at how including relational accountability alongside procedural accountability, at the centre of policy, could improve both aid relations and, in turn, the aid environment.

# Chapter 4
# Aid Policy Failings:
# Bringing in Relational Accountability

## 4.1 Introduction

Aid can play a key role in both fiscal sustainability and the delivery of public services through increasing financial flows to support a rise in investment and consumption expenditure. It can also bring important advisory support and capacity enhancement through technical assistance and sometimes policy dialogue. Alongside these benefits, though, the dependency and capacity impact that accompanies aid inflows has important, and frequently negative, implications for the recipient government. This relates to the conditionalities associated with aid and power relations.

This chapter first considers how aid policy has failed in some of its aims over the past few decades. It also considers conditionalities and how they reduce the policy space of government. Recipient government capacity is typically limited; through dependencies and transaction costs associated with the different aid modalities, perverse incentives can accompany financial flows, with vested interests influencing resource allocations. As modalities have changed over time, we consider the effectiveness of changes in participation and the interrelationship between conditionalities and aid flows.

In the second part of the chapter, we explore how a relational accountability approach could be used to rebalance the approach to aid to address some of these failings of aid policy. We discuss the revealed and hidden constraints that donors face in their aid allocations, how these vary between donor agencies and, in turn, how these determine approaches to aid policy.

Throughout this discussion we examine the impact of perverse incentives in the context of dissonance between events within the lower procedural levels of the hierarchy, and the higher, more pervasive, relational characteristics, pointing to causes of conflict resulting from discord between the two. The inclusion of elements of relational accountability could result in a different approach to the delivery of aid, one that more accurately depicts reality, and has the potential to be more effective.

### 4.2  Aid Policy Failings

Aid has achieved some important results over the past few decades. Applying the savings gap concept, it has provided governments with fiscal space and has assisted with the provision of public services. Despite this progress, and the disbursement of increasing amounts of aid in a harmonised, aligned and country-owned manner following efforts resulting from the 2005 Paris Declaration on Aid Effectiveness (OECD 2008a), aid could arguably have achieved much more. It has been limited by its failure to see its role in a fundamentally different way, and through a lack of attention to the political realities of recipient countries. The constraints under which donor agencies operate have prevented such an adjustment; in particular the need to disburse large amounts of financing has distorted incentives.

*Aid Dependency Impacts on Capacity and Transaction Costs*

Aid dependency is usually considered to be financial; that is, it relates to the share of foreign aid as a share of total revenue or of gross domestic product. Here, we consider the related issues of capacity and transaction costs, and the interplay between aid and domestic accountability.

Aid can and has made a substantial contribution in the building of capacity and institutions by easing the constraint of low revenues – as in Botswana, South Korea and Taiwan. However, it is often accompanied by high transaction costs, and it can create incentives that make it harder to overcome problems of collective action, as accountability to donors may detract from accountability to society (Brautigam and Knack 2004). Each project or agenda requires oversight and governance.

The high transaction costs arising from parallel systems present a substantial opportunity cost in terms of the quality and sustainability of outputs (World Bank 2009). The transaction costs of aid present issues of competition for both the scarce resources of government time and local skills, and the overload resulting from competition for the management of projects prevents the government from being able to effectively manage the projects and reform programmes itself. Shortages of trained staff to work on projects have, in some cases, resulted in poaching of civil servants by donors. Furthermore, the establishment of separate project units only contributes to the competition, and undermines capacity within government (Brautigam and Knack 2004). Kanbur (2000: 8) takes this argument further, considering the real cost to be the use of political capital in interacting with donors, thus 'diverting attention from domestic debate and consensus building'.

In short, there is an aid dependency trap, in terms of not only finances but also transaction costs, and therefore a high degree of investment is required in recipient governments' resources, which are diverted from issues of national policy and development. Rentier state theory, which has roots in the state creation theories discussed in Chapter 2, makes analogies between oil rents and aid inflows, finding that aid results in weak incentives to build an effective public service based on revenue collections; the vulnerability of the citizenry to political changes; and a lack of interest by the state in the welfare of citizens, and therefore a weakened accountability relationship (Moore 2001). These factors are highly dependent on the specific balance of aid modalities, to which we now turn.

## *Different Aid Modalities and Accountability*

The move towards providing foreign aid through budget support, and improvements in the design of projects both represent concerted efforts to harmonise and align aid with government systems and priorities. Indeed, budget support has been designed to improve on the weak accountability of aid through efforts to enhance information flows to service delivery units and local communities, and to build the capacity of civil society to participate in the budget preparation and implementation processes. Alongside this, there have been efforts to reduce transaction costs for government and to improve taxation collection, external auditing and anti-corruption measures. Therefore, in many respects, the shift in aid delivery modalities represents an improvement in the opportunities to provide accountability to society.

The recent move towards results-based approaches (Birdsall and Savedoff 2010) attributes more independence to the recipient government to decide how to use funds, with results rewarded regardless of how they are achieved. This shifts the risk to recipients; the risk for donors is reduced as their accountability to their constituents is facilitated by the direct linkage to results (Birdsall, Mahgoub et al. 2010, Rogerson 2011). Nonetheless, the risk of wastage and misuse of funds remains (Rogerson 2011). However, this modality implicitly assumes financial incentives are sufficient to achieve results and takes no account of the institutional constraints that may exist. Furthermore, agreement on which results are to trigger disbursement, and over what time period, brings into play the role of power in negotiation and raises a number of questions around understandings and assumptions of how progress is achieved.[1]

Despite this change in fashion, the literature highlights a number of persistent weaknesses and cases of donors diverting the accountability away from citizens. One country study observed an increase in donor projects from 800 in 1989 to 2,000 in 2002; associated with this was increased input by senior government officials in terms of facilitating such projects in the form of donor missions (Brautigam and Knack 2004: 261). Although donors recognise the problem, this does not prevent them from placing demands on limited government resources and, in some cases, poaching staff from government.

A World Bank/International Monetary Fund (IMF) (2005) review of poverty reduction strategy papers (PRSPs) identifies several factors that could increase the focus on external accountability, thereby reducing accountability to domestic citizens. These include lack of priorities, specificity and operational detail in PRSPs,

---

1    The UK's Department for International Development is trialling results-based aid (payment by results) in Ethiopia, Rwanda and Uganda.

as well as parallel processes outside domestic planning mechanisms. When placed in the context of high dependence on external assistance, donor priorities (e.g. focusing on social sectors and monitoring short-term results) can prevent the enhancement of domestic accountabilities. Based on IMF advice, donors pressure governments to increase revenue collection, resulting in a situation – at the extreme – where the government is directly accountable to donors, thus bypassing or even preventing the development of accountability with society (Gloppen and Rakner 2002).

Underlying these issues is the conditionality of aid, a concept that captures the relationship between the donor and the recipient, since requirements are imposed that can have a direct impact on both the relationship and the reform environment. Conditionality may be full or partial (as in, terms for the usage of aid accompany the financial flows, restricting the fungibility of aid; or any policy conditions that may need to be met), or 'soft', in the form of reporting or form-filling requirements to serve the donors' accountability requirements. Whichever form conditionality takes, the role of game playing and incentives becomes important. Game playing is particularly important where the fulfilment of the conditions required for disbursement would require compromising domestic political interests. Applying this analysis to the respective locations in the hierarchy of social analysis of procedural and relational accountability, this is an example of a case where events falling within the lower procedural accountability levels are discordant with the more pervasive, relational accountability structure.

*Conditionality and Donor–Recipient Relations*

The reasons for conditionality being ineffective have been thoroughly modelled and discussed (Kanbur 2000; Mosley et al. 1995; Svensson 2000, White and Morrissey 1997, Coate and Morris 1996, Adam and O'Connell 1999). Aid can, however, have the positive benefit of policy conditionalities that encourage changes such as revenue reforms and increased accountability. This depends on the extent to which international donor conditionalities are in line with domestic interests, and whether domestic influences represent accountability to the citizens, or whether rent seeking is more dominant. Here we highlight some elements of the debate that are relevant for our discussion of accountability.

The fundamental question that underlies the debate around conditionality is whether recipient governments are motivated to undertake identical reforms in the absence of conditionality. If they are, then there is no need for conditionality to enforce the reforms; therefore, the assumption underlying conditionality must be that, in the absence of policy conditions, they would not undertake the reforms. Under this assumption, even in the event of a repeated game, a recipient with a weak bargaining position can implement the conditionality on its own terms and still achieve follow-up finance, since the interests of the donor lie in disbursing funds, thus discrediting the very basis of conditionality. Four motivations for donors to disburse have been identified: avoidance of economic chaos, risked by non-receipt of aid inflows and a negative impact on the poor; political clientelism;

the risk of not servicing debt; and the career interests of aid agency personnel and the maintenance of the reputation of the agency. The close relationship between donors and recipients results in a complex and dysfunctional system and subsequent 'paper conditions' (Kanbur 2000: 6). The evidence on conditionalities has found minimal policy leverage, evidenced by the limited policy changes that are brought about and, as often quoted, points to it being a 'toothless tiger' (Killick 1995: 121).

The conditionality relationship can be seen as a series of combinations of conditionalities and disbursements and degrees of conflict between donors and recipients. Representing this as a series of game theory moves, we can distinguish three stages: 1) the negotiating process on the terms of the conditions; 2) the implementation of policies by the recipient government; and 3) the donor's response in terms of future financing (Mosley et al. 1995). As the donor aims to maximise the conditionality to achieve the desired reform for each unit of expenditure, and the recipient aims to maximise the disbursement while minimising the political cost associated with the conditionality, the bargaining strength of both players influences the outcomes.[2] Drawing from our discussions in Chapter 2, a weak and dependent state, as often found in countries reliant on foreign aid, is fiscally accountable and supervised by international organisations and donors. There are, of course, differing degrees of divergence or convergence of views between donors and recipients (White and Morrissey 1997), as well as differing short- and long-term impacts of conditionality (Coate and Morris 1996), and differing degree of representativeness of government and policy reversibility (White and Morrissey 1997). Game theory models highlight the nature and possible outcomes of the bargaining process (Kanbur 2000, Mosley et al. 1995, Svensson 2000).

Buchanan's (1975) 'Samaritan's dilemma' highlights how, as donors cannot credibly threaten to withdraw aid if the required conditions are not met, a non-representative government may be able to capture the donor in a permanent aid relationship that replicates the outcome of unconditional aid. Given the nature of the repeated game between donors and governments, they are locked into a permanent relationship that limits the effectiveness of conditionality. The donor therefore acts as the 'agency of restraint in perpetuity', preventing graduation away from aid and, by extension, preventing increased accountability to taxpayers (Adam and O'Connell 1999: 30).

The government might resist policy reform by using slippage as a strategy, agreeing to tighter *ex-ante* conditionality than it is willing to implement, as illustrated by White and Morrissey's (1997) model, Appendix 2. If there is conflict in the preference for reform, the final outcome will be a function of bargaining between the recipient and the donor. The recipient can play the game of agreeing to the tighter conditionality in a single period game knowing slippage will result. However, in a repeated game, the credibility dilemma again emerges for the donor: whether to punish slippage in accordance with the conditionality agreement, or

---

2   This is discussed in more detail in the section on power relations, in the second part of this chapter.

**Table 4.1    Donor influence through aid leverage on policy processes**

| Policy stage | Aid leverage of donor | Influences upon response of recipient |
|---|---|---|
| A. Priors (pre-existing beliefs and signalling) | Beliefs regarding effects and efficacy of policies<br>Placing specific concerns high on the agenda | Willingness to reform and alter policy choices<br>Beliefs regarding the effect of any given policy |
| B. Options | Provide and interpret information on policy options<br>Policy advice and knowledge transfer | Willingness to reform |
| C. Design | Technical assistance on elements of policy design | Ability to design reforms in terms of technical capacity |
| D. Capacity | Support for policy choice and implementation strategies<br>Taking responsibility for unpopular policies<br>Providing evidence to build support or to counter opposition | Ability to design reforms in terms of scope for political negotiation and strength of domestic opposition (for example, political and civil society) |
| E. Commitment | Financial support for adopting policies<br>Building policymaking capability | Ability to implement reforms in terms of scope for political negotiation and strength of domestic opposition |
| F. Implementation | Technical support and assistance | Ability to implement reforms<br>Whether policy choice agrees with conditions |

*Source*: Adapted and developed from Morrissey (2004).

whether to disburse anyway and increase utility. This can be seen as strategic ambiguity, whereby the government aims to maintain in its negotiation with donors (Richey 1999).

The interests of different groups within the recipient group (and also the donor group) play an important role, because the recipient groups that bear the political costs of the reforms (for example, line ministries) are often different from those involved in negotiating the agreement (for example, ministries of finance and central banks) (Mosley et al. 1995). Yet, often, the government is perceived to be a homogenous entity, whereas the reality is one of different interests and competing factions. Is there an order of decision making that influences the outcomes of a negotiation around conditionality? Applying a Stackleberg leader–follower game (Kanbur 2000), the donor (the leader) decides on the level of aid to maximise its preferences, and the government – albeit the recipient, and seemingly less powerful – influences outcomes by deciding on its responses to each level of aid. Such responses might include its fiscal response as well as its future negotiating strategy. The donor then responds to this reaction. Morrissey (2004) identifies six policy stages, some of which are not directly related to the conditionalities. The key aspect here is the choice that pertains to the recipient and the observation that conditions are not required if the donor agrees with the policy choice made by the recipient. Stages A and B, outlined in Table 4.1, correspond to willingness to reform; Stages C and D to the design of reforms; and Stages E and F to reform implementation.

Interest groups influence the choice of policies and, depending on the extent of power they possess, interact with conditionalities. Where the government is not representative, increases in aid are channelled directly to the favoured interest group (Adam and O'Connell 1999). This links back to the discussion in Chapter 3 of the complex nature of elites and the different interests to which different groups within government are responding. Rent seeking from aid may result in, and be used to maintain, power in the context of clientelism. What is the impact of uncertainty on policy reform? Stochastic (i.e. random) future tax rates could lead to both the private sector (in terms of investment) and the government (in terms of policy reform) exhibiting waiting behaviour, such as cosmetic reforms and avoiding making irreversible changes (Adam and O'Connell 1999). For example, structural adjustment programmes of the 1980s and 1990s reduced the discretion of tax policies and increased the contestability of the political system (1999). Partial implementation of reform arises as leaders implement reforms up to the point where the marginal benefit (additional resources) equals the marginal cost (constraints on autonomy) (Bates 1996, cited in Adam and O'Connell 1999). While this is an interesting analysis, it assumes procedural accountability characteristics, including those of full information and rationality.

Assuming that reform interests differ between the donor and the recipient, even in the event of a repeated game, a recipient with a weak bargaining position can implement conditionality on its own terms and still achieve follow-up finance. This is because the interests of the donor are to disburse funds, thus discrediting the very basis of conditionality. The models discussed above, with their different focuses – including the bargaining process (Kanbur 2000, Mosley et al. 1995, Svensson 2000) and the extent of conflict existing around reforms (White and Morrissey 1997); the time horizons involved (Coate and Morris 1996); and repeated games (Adam and O'Connell 1999) – illustrate how conditionality is often ineffective.

In terms of the influence on the accountability relationship, game theory approaches present useful analyses of the interaction between donors and governments, which, in turn, aid understanding of how this relationship shapes the local accountability relationship between the state and society. Again, this highlights the interaction between the procedural and the relational levels of accountability. Understanding why conditionality has not worked can also be considered in terms of conflict within Williamson's hierarchy. Where the lower-level procedural framework is discordant with the higher-level relational characteristics, negotiation and manoeuvring must take place around formal and contractual, procedural performance measures: the more pervasive relational structure results in adjustments to the lower-level procedural assessments of performance, to enable aid to be disbursed. This is borne out in the international aid market, which African governments play with skill (Chabal and Daloz 1999).

### 4.3 Bringing in Relational Accountability

Relational accountability has a number of attributes that have the potential to overcome some of the failings described above. As these involve a different way of conceptualising the donor–recipient relationship, they also require a radically different approach to aid delivery. Key aspects of relational accountability (those we deconstructed in Chapter 3) that are important for this new approach include a comprehensive analysis of the highly context-specific and complex cultural factors that underlie the relationships around which accountability is formed. The accountability outcomes are the specific result of political and social relations based on the interplay between actors and social institutions.

As Chapter 3 noted, procedural accountability and relational accountability embody different understandings of power. Looking through the procedural accountability lens, power is a limited contractual resource, resting with either the principal or the agent. However, from the relational accountability perspective, power results from the specific cultural and political history. It is a fluid process that underpins all interactions, is subtly demonstrated through language, and is unlimited.

It is essential to understand how donors' view of power is, on the surface, mismatched with how power actually operates in recipient governments. Donors tend to overlook the informal institutions important in the government's sourcing of power. Indeed, understanding relational accountability means understanding politics, and applying that understanding, which is outside the public administration arena of donor discourse. Although relational characteristics may be present in government institutions of many countries, both developing and developed, actors' different perceptions of power, associated with their societal context of origin, have an impact on their behaviour in any negotiation process. In an attempt to understand the context in developing countries, the inappropriate imposition of 'Western' understandings of concepts such as civil society (as discussed in Chapter 2), can often inhibit progress in the aid relationship.

*Donors' Foreign Policy and How Conflict Arises*

We can identify some commonalities in the development discourse, yet each donor has specific foreign policy objectives that result in the dominance of different styles of aid delivery and specific interests. The changing aid landscape has seen a rise in donors outside the Organisation for Economic Co-operation and Development's Development Assistance Committee (OECD-DAC), as well as a changing geopolitics that sees African countries acting as donors to China

(Hu 2013). The language of development from OECD-DAC donors is focused on poverty reduction as captured in the Millennium Development Goals, and aims for ownership, partnership and aid effectiveness. The UK legislated to establish a 'core power', whereby all development assistance (excluding contributions to multilaterals, overseas territories and humanitarian relief) has to contribute to poverty reduction: a restriction that is strongly procedural in nature (DFID 2002).

There is, perhaps, a dissonance between the rhetoric for the provision of aid and the real motivations. One common foreign policy objective is stability, such that disturbances or violence are avoided because they risk disrupting economic interests. A second is protecting and enhancing coalitions of investment that are in the donors' interests. The separation of these political domestic and security concerns from the disbursement of aid varies among different donors. Bilaterals and multilaterals have a different approach, as do the two broad groups of OECD-DAC donors (and, within this, the European donors) and other donors (including the BRICS – Brazil, Russia, India, China and South Africa – and others including Japan and South Korea).[3] Perhaps the most fundamental separation in approach between the OECD-DAC donors and other donors is related to the role of democracy and the state in development, as explained below.

Whilst higher-level political interests are implicitly connected through aid being related to influence, the explicit aim of foreign aid among OECD-DAC donors is to pursue policy objectives in line with both poverty reduction and the international aid agenda and, in doing so, to ensure the disbursement of increasing amounts of aid in a harmonised manner. This agenda has involved a movement towards a more formalised aid relationship, along the lines drawn in the Paris Declaration and the Accra Agenda for Action, which is firmly located within the procedural levels of Williamson's hierarchy, and takes no account of the higher-level influences of relational accountability. An example of this is the Accra website, which, in a rather paternalistic tone, states that 'developing countries are committing to take control of their own futures' (OECD 2008b) and pursues the same results-focused and alignment issues as the Paris Declaration: ownership; country systems; untying aid; South–South cooperation; transparency and accountability; conditionality; and predictability (Eurodad 2008).

Most OECD-DAC donors base development on a liberal model of democracy and good governance, as enshrined in the Washington Consensus. The increasingly mainstream governance discourse looks at the importance of politics and questions what underlies formal institutions. However, perceptions of rent seeking, clientelism and associated characteristics persist as 'pathologies' (Unsworth 2010: 6). The two core foreign policy objectives of security and domestic investment highlighted

---

3    They are referred to here as other donors, as an alternative to the common emerging term 'new donors'. This is to explicitly recognise that they have in fact acted as donors for decades in some cases (China to Africa, Russia to China, as well as UAE, Saudi Arabia and Kuwait who have been donors for around 40 years). Roles as donors or recipients rather reflects shifting geopolitics.

above remain unreconciled with the rhetoric of aid of traditional donors. This dichotomy underpins the conflict in aid relationships.

The increase in aid from other donors has been substantial since 2000. Provisional data point to non-DAC donors amounting in aggregate to one third of all development assistance flows in 2009, and having increased ten-fold during the decade (Greenhill et al. 2013). This finance has largely been sought from recipient governments due to its speed and cost effectiveness. It appears to have increased recipients' bargaining power with OECD-DAC donors and to have reduced effectiveness of conditionality, as we would expect from the discussion above. These other donors do not face such a dichotomy between the rhetoric of aid and their foreign policy objectives. An East Asian model (involving China, Japan and South Korea) is emerging that offers a balance to the dominance of Northern and Western approaches (Urban et al. 2011b).[4] Of particular note and increasing recent interest is the approach of China.[5] China's lack of interest in the good governance agenda stems from a view of development that places the focus on the socioeconomic conditions of the social group, rather than on the individual through democratisation (Ampiah and Naidu 2008). It also considers routes to development as being specific to each country's socioeconomic context (Urban et al. 2011a). Subsequently, it claims to have no interest in the politics of the recipient government.

China bundles aid with trade and other investment (Urban et al. 2011a), proposing no expertise or interest in the soft skills of capacity building or assisting policy dialogue.[6] Rather, the input is financial, with a focus on infrastructure, often providing the resources to build such infrastructure directly and, through this, more efficiently overcoming any capacity gaps that would present challenges to the delivery of the investment. Although support is offered as no strings attached (Lagerkvist, 2009) a link can be seen between transport infrastructure and access to natural resources to serve China's growing demand, demonstrating a direct commercial interest (de Haan and Warmerdam 2012) and supported by their high investments in the infrastructure sector (Greenhill et al 2013). Of most interest here is the way that China presents itself strategically to support a new geopolitical settlement that looks to Asia. China's aid aims to support partnership and is delivered without policy advice or conditionalities, apart from requiring recognition of the One-China policy and an implicit deference to Chinese leadership (de Haan and Warmerdam 2012, Urban et al. 2011b).[7] While the approach might be seen as rigid

---

4    We note that Korea is an OECD-DAC member, but also shows characteristics of the East Asian model.

5    China has an aid programme of USD 5bn per year, that is growing at around 20 per cent and almost USD 60 bn of foreign direct investment in 2011 was directed to developing countries (UNDP 2012).

6    Professor Li Xiaoyun, 'Old puzzles, new pieces: development cooperation in tomorrow's world', ODI CAPE Conference, November 2012.

7    Exemplified by the Forum on China-Africa Cooperation (FOCAC) http://www.focac.org/eng/

there is evidence of different approaches being taken where necessary (de Haan and Warmerdam 2012, regarding Sudan in the early 1980s).

Locating this approach in the procedural–relational accountability framework, the East operates more strongly within the relational accountability realm. The bundling of interests represents an 'intended ambiguity [with] no clear distinction between aid and investment, no clear distinction between state-owned and private enterprises and also an ambiguity in leadership and accountability of the 'aid industry' (Urban et al 2011b: 21). However, we must look beyond this revealed degree of separation between politics and aid, and acknowledge the unrevealed incentives. Donors' incentives to disburse aid can also include *paternalism*, that is, donors believing they know what is best for the recipient (Collier and Gunning 1996, cited in White and Morrissey 1997: 498), furthering the career interests of aid agency personnel and maintaining the reputation of the agency (Kanbur 2000).

A major constraint in OECD-DAC donors' aid policy is the need to account to domestic constituents for aid spending. Since the economic downturn in developed countries in 2009, increasing domestic political pressures have been requiring the demonstration of the efficacy of aid to donor taxpayers. This has led to an increasing focus on quick and demonstrable results, which has encouraged unrealistic expectations of the speed with which aid can achieve results. The corresponding short-term-focused results agenda limits the flexibility needed to work towards achieving more sustainable results over the longer term. Due to the pressure to achieve results in the short term, donors are unable to address the inherent complexities that are necessary to overcome governance constraints to delivering public goods. Approaches such as facilitation, or employing flexibility to respond to changes in circumstances, which may even involve delaying results, can help to address such constraints (see Tavakoli et al. 2013). Although some donors (including the UK, Sweden and Norway) have acknowledged the importance of working informally, it is easier to disburse aid to formal systems and institutions, particularly given the pressure to disburse large amounts of aid (O'Neill, et al 2007).

What does this theory imply for how aid policy could be adjusted to be more effective? Conceding to the constraint imposed by domestic constituents avoids conflict. As procedural accountability exists within the broader concept of relational accountability (which has a deeper and more durable structure, and is located at the higher level of Williamson's hierarchy), relational accountability therefore provides the framework within which procedural accountability can function. As we have seen, if an occurrence arises through procedural accountability that does not fit within the boundaries of the higher-level relational accountability, then discord results, and this is what often leads to conflict in the form of game playing. The tension between the need for adjustment could result in either rejection of the procedural accountability demand or a shift in the relational accountability part of the framework.

*Recommended New Policy*

This book's model of accountability focuses on the central government public sector and how the public sector interacts with the international development community through the delivery of budget support. In the international aid environment, actors from different cultures operating within a non-Western societal context meet (Chapter 6 applies the model to the aid context in Tanzania). Here, we can see the interaction and mutual dependency of the two types of accountability: procedural accountability is imposed as a tool through which donors understand the development context, embodied in processes; however, its operation is tempered by the relational accountability context and methods, and therefore a relational lens must also be adopted to enable a full understanding. Aid needs to reflect the institutional context in recipient countries. A new approach should take into account the constraints associated with relational concerns; and also deconstruct and recognise the accountability constraints upon donors, which in turn make these proposed changes challenging to implement, as we will explore in Chapter 7.

## 4.4 Summary: Aid Policy, Unrevealed Incentives and Constraints

The failure of conditionality to effect policy reform is well understood, and strategies – such as strategic ambiguity (Richey 1999) and slippage – have been observed. An important conclusion is that policy conditionalities can encourage reforms where they are aligned with domestic interests – although this calls into question the entire premise for the conditions. Neither government nor donors are homogenous and appreciation of different interest groups and their differential ability to exercise power allows us to understand how aid has a role in rent seeking. Where the government is not representative and operates in a clientelistic context, elites may use aid as one of the financing sources for rents that are distributed to maintain power.

Donors' view of power often appears to be mismatched with how power actually operates in recipient governments because they overlook the informal institutions important in the government's sourcing of power. This has an impact on the negotiation process around conditionalities. The inappropriate imposition of 'Western' understandings of concepts, such as civil society (as discussed in Chapter 2), can often inhibit the development of an understanding between donors and recipients. The relational understanding of power assumes that donors should understand the socio-political context of the recipient country.

We saw in the discussion of donors' foreign policy that the constraints experienced by East Asian donors are very different from the OECD-DAC group. Although not representative of the East Asian group, China, for example, does not engage in the good governance agenda but, rather, has a pragmatic commercial and investment interest to help meet its internal demand for natural resources. This sits in sharp contrast to the liberal model of democracy and good governance that underpins the development vision of OECD-DAC donors.

Looking beyond the revealed separation between politics and aid to the unrevealed incentives to disburse aid that include paternalism and the two core foreign policy objectives of security and domestic investment, we can see how relational accountability may be in conflict with procedural accountability. Aid could be more effective if donors were released from the need to respond to constraints that they face. This is of course an unrealistic expectation, since, just as recipients face challenges brought by their political economy, so do donors. The latter are, however, infrequently examined; to consider donors more explicitly would enrich our understanding of the limitations of aid policy, and enable the potential to adjust expectations to more realistic levels. This could reduce the conflict that results from discord between events within the procedural levels, and the higher, more pervasive, relational levels, of Williamson's hierarchy. More explicitly, including relational accountability elements could result in a different approach to the delivery of aid, one that more accurately depicts reality and has the potential to be more effective. In short, a relational accountability approach, alongside procedural accountability, could rebalance aid to address some of these failings of aid policy.

Developing a new model of accountability depends on understanding the views of those involved in accountability relationships and their relationships with civil society representatives and agencies of the state. To do this requires a specific epistemology (discussed in Appendix 1), which is applied in Chapters 5 and 6.

# Chapter 5

# The Accountability Context in Tanzania

## 5.1 Introduction

In Chapters 2 and 3, we analysed the procedural and relational forms of accountability. In Chapter 3, we saw that there is a need for relational accountability to allow for the existence of contradictory political and social relations, based on implicit, informal and accidental rules. We understood how accountability is embodied within the personal relations between agents, who interact with the social structure. Elites are placed at the core of the analysis, given the pivotal role this group plays in influencing policies and decisions and linking state and society. The reach of accountability from this core stretches out in a web-like structure, capturing actors as they function within a multitude of different social roles within elite networks

Using this understanding of accountability, we now analyse the sociopolitical context in Tanzania. We present a brief summary of modern periods in political and economic history and an analysis of the party and agencies of state. Within this context, we then analyse how societal accountability operates, and the impact of the interface between state and society on the demand and supply of accountability, examining the interaction between the procedural and relational levels of the accountability framework.

When considering accountability in the interface between state and society, we need to look at what the focus of accountability is. Either directly, or through alleviating fiscal constraints, aid aims to assist in the provision of social services, infrastructure and productive services, and budget support has traditionally directed monitoring and policy efforts towards the first of these. Accountability can therefore be discussed in the context of public-service delivery (and the central government's role in this through the mechanisms of democracy); capacity to manage public finances and other aspects of accountability (including the media); and, in turn, how civil society interfaces with these.

## 5.2 Political Institutions and Democracy

Political institutions in Tanzania have evolved from the tight control exhibited when the country was a one-party state; the strength of the ruling coalition has allowed Tanzania to enjoy a relatively stable political settlement since independence in 1961.[1] The strength of the ruling party, Chama Cha Mapinduzi (CCM, Party of the Revolution), comes from its historical roots, and from when the control exercised by President Julius Nyerere via the party ranged over both the economy and society. Hyden (1994) notes the positive correlation between Nyerere's support for the party and the resources available to him for political patronage. The president allocated ministerial positions, and ministers' interests lay primarily in securing their position in office, rather than in the longer-term goals of the party (Pinkney 1997). The formation of CCM involved a consolidation of positions, such that certain people came to hold parallel positions in the party and in government (Baregu 1994, Berg-Schlosser and Siegler 1990, Coulson 1982, Hyden 1994, Pinkney 1997), and instances of repression increased. This, in turn, may have further supported and widened the circle of political patronage. A *replenishment* of elites took place; it is possible that there was a *circulation* of elites, but it was on party terms, whereby the electorate could reject the first choice of the party, but the party could also reject the voters' choice (Pinkney 1997: 99). This can be situated within the relational accountability framework: personal relations and networks played a central function in an informal structure.

Public administration reforms of the 1980s, stimulated by a fiscal crisis (and the International Monetary Fund's Economic Recovery Programme), included the revoking of the Leadership Code, which had allowed bureaucrats to earn a second income (Costello 1996). During this period, the party played an ideological function, because the power of the civil service was strengthened, resulting in a weakened party, with reduced capacity, legitimacy and ability to define policy. This was part of the form of socialism known as *ujamaa* (emphasising the extended family and the situation of people within communities), which was signalled by the gradual replacement of the political arm by the administrative function, as the power of officials increased (Costello 1996, Pinkney 1997). This, and other crises involved 'uneven liberalisation ... which weakened the ruling coalition and enabled more entrepreneurs to emerge' (Therkildsen and Bourgouin 2012: 11). This perhaps marked the start of the increase in procedural accountability, as performance management measures were turned to as part of the focus on improving public auditing, limiting subsidies to parastatals, increasing taxes, and introducing a more realistic pricing system (Berg-Schlosser and Siegler 1990).

In Tanzania's history the party and the government have mainly been reconciled with the head of state also being the head of the party, allowing full and unified control of the country.[2] Moreover, civil society was controlled to maintain the balance of power (along the lines of Gramsci (1971) as discussed in Chapter 3). CCM's representativeness effectively declined through its attempts to increase centralisation. This was legitimised by multiparty democracy, which

---

1    The ruling coalition comprises the ruling elite and their supporters (Therkildsen and Bourgouin 2012).

2    The roles were briefly separated between 1995 and 1997 when Mwinyi retained the party chairperson after handing over the presidency to Mkapa.

allowed it to maintain its claim as the preferred party, despite this decline in representativeness (Costello 1996). The movement towards multiparty politics followed recommendations in the 1992 Nyalali Report and, by the end of 1993, 12 political parties had been approved (Chege 1994, Hyden 1994), with the first multiparty elections taking place in 1995. However, the context was tightly centrally controlled, and the domination of CCM continued.

Next, we will consider how accountability has variously operated through the ruling party, and how challenges from the opposition have influenced this political landscape.

*Political Power Bases, Factions and Competition*

Until recently, CCM's dominance has continued (Khan and Gray 2006). The failure of the large number of opposition parties to unite against CCM illustrated the party's success at limiting the mobilisation of society, through both the marginalisation of civil society and the operation of networks of relational accountability. This influence is shored up by media support for CCM; election financing; the use of public resources for campaigning; the state security apparatus favouring CCM; legislative restrictions on forming coalitions; the banning of independent candidacy; and special seat allocations. In addition, the costs of participating in elections have increased (Kelsall and Mmuya 2005), raising the importance of financing from the private sector, and the integration of business and politics. CCM's dominance until recent years has been possible as a result of CCM's ability to use the enduring country-wide structure of local networks (Mmuya 1998) established in the early post-independence era, for communication and patronage purposes. This social base 'cuts across regional, ethic and social divides' (Therkildsen and Bourgouin 2012: 14).

Additionally, the electoral advantages CCM maintains over opposition parties include those related to access to finance, as political party fund allocations are based on the number of seats won (UNDP 2007, Therkildsen and Bourgouin 2012). The Political Parties Act regulates funding and its ruling is that a parliamentary seat is accompanied with a government subsidy. Therkildsen and Bourgouin (2012: 40, citing Sokomani 2005) note the difference in ruling-party and opposition monthly subventions after the 2000 elections, when each month the ruling party drew USD547,000, over ten times more than all opposition parties combined. This is further supplemented by CCM membership fees and business ownership, with CCM owning *Uhuru* the Kiswahili newspaper, companies, real estate and sports arenas (Ewald 2011).

The electoral system is structured such that the incumbent has the advantage through clientelism and the network of elites that maintain power through CCM support, oiling the wheels of everyday life from tax payments to business registration and property ownership. The military is an important member of the ruling coalition and there are strong affiliations between the party and the army (which offers sources of rents). The army used to be required to be CCM members.

An example of this connection is President Jakaya Kikwete who was elected in 2005 and in office for two terms totalling ten years. He spent 16 formative years in the military, retiring as Lieutenant-Colonel and, during his time in the army, he tried to bring the army closer to politics. The intelligence service plays an active but covert role in both political and senior civil-service appointments, and through this has political influence. It also has had a range of commercial investments through the commercial arm of the National Service (SUMA-JKT): these include Meremeta gold mine, a rice farm, furniture processing and livestock keeping enterprises. It supplies tractors and power tillers, directly supporting Kilimo Kwanza (the government's Agriculture First strategy).[3]

The bureaucracy is another arm and power base of the party. The relationship between the executive and the senior civil service is controlled closely by the presidency, the chair of CCM. Senior ranks of the civil service are controlled, ensuring that the enactment of policy supports the interests of the party. The president appoints, promotes, terminates, transfers and has the power to revoke appointments for the following: Chief Secretary (the head of the civil service and Secretary to the Cabinet); Permanent Secretaries and their deputies; Heads of extra-ministerial/independent departments; Regional Administrative Secretaries; Regional and District Commissioners; High Commissioners and Ambassadors; members of the Public Service Commission; and so on (Bana and McCourt 2006). The reach of the party to the district and village council employees is an important mechanism for ensuring support and, despite the lack of success in decentralisation reforms, there has been some increased power for local authorities in the implementation of policies (Therkildsen and Bourgouin 2012). They found interview evidence that civil-service transfers and sackings may even be linked to success in mobilising votes, and indications that performance reviews are undertaken by the party to monitor this (Therkildsen and Bourgouin 2012).

This relationship, between bureaucracy and party, has increased over time, with a recent reduction in the number of technically competent senior officials at the same time as the number of positions that are politically appointed by Kikwete has grown: 'Senior government posts are routinely awarded on patronage grounds, for example, the former Minister of Finance, and current Director of Public Prosecutions and the Attorney General' (Cooksey 2011: 93). Although this influence is strong, factional conflict and power struggles between groups of civil-service staff reduce it below its potential, leading to inefficiency in policy implementation. This is because political appointments, particularly those of key

---

3   Meremeta gold mine received funds from the external payment account (EPA) corruption scandal in 2012 (Therkildsen 2011). Jeetu Patel, a prominent Asian–Tanzanian businessman, is licensed to import power tillers and has been implicated in the EPA case (Therkildsen and Bourgouin 2012, Therkildsen 2011). Furthermore, in January 2012 it was reported that the government ordered district councils to purchase at least 50 tractors each and sell them on to farmers (Saiboko 2012).

senior government officials, present opportunities for those in power to allocate public resources to support their own key interests.

Ruling party membership, or even simply the flying of a CCM flag, can have an impact on personal and business affairs, from dealings with the revenue authority to land registration and licensing. Conversely, the same mechanisms can be used negatively:

> Intimidation in Tanzania is not physical, they use other ways. For example, they [the government] look at tax returns and send out a higher bill. It is therefore legal but there are different triggers. (Interview with head of civil-society organisation, July 2009(2))

> Gagging is sophisticated. They [the opposition and outspoken CCM politicians] are given space so that they don't revolt but no change is allowed. (Interview with head of civil-society organisation, July 2009)

The legitimacy gained through ostensible democracy has been associated with an increased influence of state elites. The *state class* comprises members of the political, administrative and economic elite, who have increased in number since the 1960s, and corresponds to the understanding of elites discussed in Chapter 3, stressing the importance of networks, influence and co-optation.

While the democratic system has become more open, and checks and balances on the executive have increased, efforts to suppress opposition parties persist. Since the introduction of multipartyism in 1992, 18 new parties have been formed, and 12 are currently registered, although only six are represented in Parliament (National Electoral Commission,[4] Tripp 2012). There are few parties in Parliament due to frequent co-optation by CCM and laws prohibiting coalitions being formed. They 'are harassed and kept busy in court for minor injunctions, misdemeanours and trespassing violations' (2012: 7).

Chama cha Demokrasia na Maendeleo (the Party of Democracy and Development, CHADEMA) is now the main opposition party on the mainland and, in 2010, a presidential candidate from the opposition gained almost a third of the votes: the first time since 1995. The opposition have increasingly contributed to a lively parliamentary debate, by setting the agenda and initiating motions and in doing so have pushed forward the reforms of the legislature. An opposition challenge to CCM hegemony is anticipated, without there being much real threat, although this increasingly visible role of the opposition on the mainland has stimulated changes within CCM (Therkildsen and Bourgouin 2012). Tanzania has historically experienced high turnout in elections, averaging 79 per cent in the previous three elections but falling to 43 per cent in 2010 (National Electoral

---

4    National Electoral Commission www.nec.go.tz/ and http://www.tanzania.go.tz/ tumeuchaguzi.html.

Commission cited in Policy Forum 2011: 4, Governance Working Group 2010) suggesting voter disillusionment alongside opposition complaints of vote rigging.[5]

President Benjamin Mkapa pursued a reformist and neoliberal agenda between 1995 and 2005, bringing together the political and business elites (Shivji 2006) and increasing the importance of the private sector in the patronage relationship (Kelsall 2002). This period involved an *internationalisation,* through a commitment to the neoliberal agenda of the international financial institutions. This bringing together of the political and business elites can be considered the evolution of the 'circle of trust' in the relational accountability perspective. It is only recently that political stability and patterns of rent seeking have begun to change. The different groups and influences within CCM have changed gradually, and the decline in the socialist clique has been accompanied by a growth in the free marketers since the early 1990s. One strategy for political stabilisation has been to ensure different factions of similar levels of bargaining power are kept within CCM (Khan and Gray 2006).[6]

Until around 2005, the party whip kept tight control over members and decisions took place outside parliament in small groups (Mmuya 1998). More recently, however, increasing fragmentation has become apparent as opposition from CCM factions has become more visible:

> The chief whip has become more relaxed with the recent reforms. Before, he would find a way to stop negative talk against the government but now that ufasidi [corruption] is in the open there are fewer sensitive issues to uncover. The executive is still powerful and uses its power to give or to limit freedom.
> (Interview with backbench CCM MP and head of a parastatal, June 2009)

The increasing prominence of the opposition has supported these CCM factions as they are provided with a credible route for defection, increasing their bargaining power and, in turn, their ability to both demand and seek rents (Kelsall et al. 2013). These separatist tendencies have therefore been supported by an incentive to tolerate rent seeking and the growth of capitalism within CCM. As we will see below, CCM has successfully co-opted businesses such that party endorsement facilitates business establishment and operation and, in turn, provides rents for the party. The continued dominance and control of CCM gives the appearance of centralised power (Khan and Gray 2006), although closer and more recent examination reveals tussling, uncoordinated bargaining and the importance of rents in maintaining a balance of power among the different factions and, consequently, stability. The apparent centralisation of power is masking tensions between different factions:

---

5    There have been calls for an independent electoral commission since the start of multipartyism (Tripp 2012).

6    A recent example of this was the inability of the breakaway political party Chama Cha Jamii (CCJ) (the Party of Society) to register ahead of the 2010 elections.

[T]he diffuse power structure within the CCM leads to the appearance of centralized power in Tanzania, as there appear to be few solid blocks of opposition within the party ... while factions are weak, so is the central power, and it is difficult for the leadership to override internal factions that emerge on an ad hoc basis when big rents and transfers are at stake. (Khan and Gray 2006: 53)

As discussed in Chapter 3, the effectiveness of centralised power depends on the balance between the strength of the competing factions in relation to the leadership's ability to centralise power directly. While this balance has fluctuated during different periods of Tanzania's recent history, the common pattern is one of a weak leadership and continued competition for rents.

*The Legislature*

What is the culture of the Tanzanian parliament, and how has this interacted with the emergence of democracy? The dominant culture places importance on the approaches of individual members of parliament (MPs), and has impacted their accountability, as well as affecting the accountability checks and balances that parliament can effect on the executive (Hyden 2010). CCM can be considered to have a hierarchical party culture, where leadership of the party is strong, with procedures being used to maintain discipline. Party interests are served and deliberations often take place in exclusive groups. Although there is high and increasing scope for debate within CCM, there is a limit on the autonomy of MPs (Hyden 2010). An example comes from the extractive industries, where incentives to remain loyal and to focus on 'rubber stamping legislation' result in most well-informed CCM MPs neither opposing government policy nor proposing contradictory legislation (Mejia Acosta 2013: 18). This means strong loyalty, but a weak deliberative process, with a minority group setting the party interests that prevail. Although CCM is well organised and internally democratic, it has lost control in parliament over time (Mejia Acosta 2013).

While the executive has remained strong, the power of parliament was reduced in the 1977 constitution, and it became subordinate to the party and the presidency (Mihyo 1994, cited in Olowu 2000: 159, Okumu and Holmquist 1984). Parliament is constrained by weak capacity. In recent decades, parliament has had only a short time for deliberation, lacked free access to information, been dependent on the executive for transport, income, information and influence, and has provided no training for MPs. In short, the parliament has not functioned as a forum for debate, as MPs have not felt free to speak their minds; instead, matters of national debate have been discussed by the party behind closed doors (Coulson 1982, Khan and Gray 2006).

To fulfil its representative function more effectively, it requires both elected representation and greater technical capacity. Recent reforms have been championed by Samuel Sitta, the Speaker of the National Assembly (2005–2010). These include granting an independent budget for parliament; three oversight

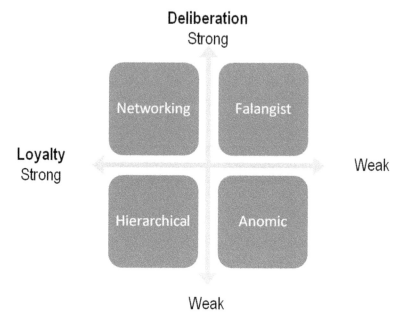

**Figure 5.1     Types of party culture**

*Source:* Hyden, G. (2010).

committees that are chaired by opposition MPs (the Parliamentary Accounts Committee, the Local Authorities Accounts Committee and the Parastatal and Other Bodies Committee, now merged with the Parliamentary Accounts Committee); the extension of parliamentary sessions; and ensuring the impartiality of the Speaker (OPM 2005, UNDP 2007, Sitta et al. 2008, Tripp 2012, Interview with Samuel Sitta, June 2009). An increased awareness of waste and people not being held to account, increasing education levels and natural resource wealth, and the need to maintain legitimacy as competition for power between factions and the leadership increases, have presented a window of opportunity for these changes. The separation of powers was the first and perhaps most significant change. In the Parliamentary Administration Act of 2008 the parliament was granted its own budget and independent staff that, rather than being members of the civil service, now accounts directly to parliament. Almost three quarters of those surveyed thought that opposition parties were now having a greater impact in parliament than previously (URT 2012a).[7] Since parliament was effectively appended to the executive for many years, there was, predictably, resistance to these changes:

---

7    Findings from The Views Of the People survey and focus groups that took place in eleven mainland regions between January and March 2012. Approximately 440 people participated in focus groups nationwide. Results were weighted to provide an approximate national picture (URT 2012a).

They [the reforms] have been resisted, naturally.to start with. After years of a parliament that was thought to be part of an appendix to the executive, all these measures brought considerable resistance ... this is all tied up with the fact that a speaker was to come from a political party and some of the top members of government in parliament occupy central committee positions in the party. So I had quite a few instances where it looked like I would be disciplined by the party and though the speaker has to come from a political party, they can easily get rid of you. But ... in November 2007 we changed the rules so that it said clearly in the rules of the house that the speaker must be impartial. (Interview with Speaker of the National Assembly (2005–2010), Samuel Sitta, June 2009)

More budget information is now available to MPs, non-governmental organisations and the media, and there are greater opportunities for MP and civil-society involvement in the process, as well as some marginal increase in capacity and assertiveness, especially in the oversight committees chaired by opposition MPs: the Parliamentary Accounts Committee and the Local Authorities Accounts Committee.[8] Several special committees have been established, and their investigations of the external payment account (EPA) and Richmond corruption cases have demonstrated parliament's increased influence since 2000.[9] Nevertheless, knowledge of key aspects of the budget process is still lacking, resulting in limited scrutiny and very few actual challenges to the budget, allowing reallocations for patronage purposes to persist. Hence, 'The ability of the National Assembly to question or influence sectoral allocations and to ensure that they follow sectoral policies is therefore very limited. The technical capacity of the sectoral committees is also limited' (Public Financial Management Working Group 2009: 42). The current Speaker of the National Assembly, Anne Makinda, has not continued to support a challenge coalition of critical and vocal MPs. This has reduced the reform momentum in parliament. The strength of the executive and weakness of parliament has been facilitated by the dominance of the ruling party, as the executive uses parliament to support its own agenda, often providing endorsement for its views. Next, we will consider how political elites and their connections with business elites further support the ruling coalition.

---

8   The World Bank has supported the training of MPs.

9   The External Payment Account (EPA) corruption case relates to payments to 22 local companies that were made from the account in 2005/06. The total value of payments made from the account during the fiscal year was Tshs 133bn (approximately USD 103m), of which 68 per cent have been found to be based on '*invalid or fraudulent supporting documents*' (Controller and Auditor General 2008: 15). In 2008/09, budget-support disbursements equivalent to 12 per cent of the budget were delayed by three months as donors requested responses to questions concerning the follow up of the auditors recommendations (ThisDay 2008a, 2008b, United Republic of Tanzania 2008).

*Political Elites and the Private Sector*

CCM has financial advantages over opposition parties and its direct ownership of businesses offers sources of finance and influence. Linkages between the private commercial sector and politicians are important sources of revenue, both through tax revenues, as discussed in Chapter 6, and through rents. Business–political relationships are robust in Tanzania; they have remained untouched by governance reforms and have even increased in recent years, as increased political competition both within and between parties has required more resources to participate at all levels (including the lower factions, which have been increasing in prominence). MPs are themselves often powerful businessmen and 'businessmen have become active in lobbying politicians and bureaucrats for individual advantages' (Cooksey 2011: 69). Both Mkapa and Kikwete had powerful businessman acting as their campaign managers (Cooksey 2011, Kelsall et al. 2013). For the individual candidate, participating in an election is an expensive endeavour: *brown envelope* contributions are required at all stages of the nomination process, such that participating in the nomination process costs at least Tsh 10 million (approximately £4000 in 2012).[10] This has increased the interdependency of the business–politics relationship. Over half of people surveyed considered there was now an increased incidence of politicians buying votes during elections (URT 2012a).

Alongside increasing political competition prompting searches for finance, as politics and the economy have become increasingly liberalised the relationships between business and politics have developed over time. During *ujamaa*, rent creation was coordinated and focused on national development but, from the 1990s onwards, it became increasingly uncoordinated and chaotic, 'increasingly favouring private actors … in particular formerly marginalised Asian merchant capitalists' (Cooksey 2011: 13, 19). However, the commercial sector is widely known to be weakly organised. Commercial actors do not organise themselves collectively; instead they predominantly interact with government and politicians individually, which highlights the importance of the informal and the personal.[11]

The government from 2005 onwards is widely understood to have been captive to an interest group, known as *mtandao* (a network), which developed, from 1995, to support Kikwete's election as president. Support and financing were offered during the 2005 election and the reshuffling of positions occurred subsequently:

---

10    Interview with a candidate who participated in the CCM nomination process, August 2012.

11    The Tanzania Private Sector Foundation and the Tanzanian National Business Council are both donor supported fora that represent other bodies including the Tanzania Chamber of Commerce, Industry and Agriculture, the Confederation of Tanzanian Industries, the Tanzania Chamber of Mines and Energy and the Tourism Confederation of Tanzania (although the latter three recently withdrew their membership) (Therkildsen and Bourgouin 2012).

The problem is what to do with the mtandao post-election, as they all had high expectations for ministerial and parliamentary posts. They are powerful people and some won seats themselves. Kikwete shook off some but others still expect repayment. (Interview with head of opposition party, June 2009)

[The high-level corruption case] Richmond was about politics not corruption. It was used to get rid of people from Kikwete's mtandao. (Interview with director of state agency, July 2009)

Parliamentary sources say these four individuals [Lowassa, Rostam Aziz, Chenge and Makamba] are seen as the main players in a network of politicians which has forged a particularly-powerful alliance within the ruling party over the past decade or so ... CCM legislators are now sharply divided in three distinct groups – those who support [this] alliance, those who oppose it, and those who are basically neutral. (ThisDay 2009a)

The inward focus of President Kikwete's presidency is partly a result of this *mtandao* that supported his 2005 election win. The nature of relational accountability is that such support would implicitly require reciprocity and pay-offs. Examples of opportunities for these in policymaking can be seen in the content of the Kilimo Kwanza (Agriculture First) policy, launched in 2009, and the movement towards resurrecting the Arusha Declaration. Kilimo Kwanza was the first agricultural policy to privilege the private sector and to promote joint ventures with foreign investors, encouraging 'large-scale commercial agriculture' (Cooksey 2012: 24). It also continued the strengthening of cooperatives that started under Mkapa, and increased the state role in planning for the agriculture sector (CCM 2010). As the 2010 election saw reduced support for both CCM and Kikwete, it was followed by increased competition for rents and control. The subsequent resignation of the Central Committee, its Secretary General and secretariat in April 2011 released Kikwete from the *mtandao*.

Overall, Kikwete's first term – from 2005 to 2010 – involved increased voice and reduced pursuit of liberalisation, and represented a period of domestic *vocalisation*. Politicians purchased newspapers and radio stations, encouraging the expansion of the media. This is a symptom of increased competition for power between the leadership and factions within the inner core of elites, and, arguably, this increased vocalisation was necessary to allow for the continued legitimacy of the party. Kikwete's second term (2010–2015) started with a reduced CCM parliamentary and presidential majority, after low electoral turnout. This may signify increasing voter disillusionment, disenfranchisement and intimidation, and suggests a need for CCM to seek legitimacy in another form if it is to stay in power.[12] If reciprocity was the primary motivation for such an inward focus in

---

12    Kikwete secured 60.4 per cent in the parliamentary elections and 61.2 per cent in the presidential elections. Turnout was 42.9 per cent, well below the average of 77.8 per

his first term, increased freedom from the need to service clientelistic networks in his second term presents an opportunity for the pursuit of more reformist and outward-looking policies. Although a reformist stance has not been in evidence, the drive to ensure CCM's legacy in the 2015 elections may have prompted some proactive ministers being put in prominent positions during the May 2012 cabinet reshuffle, and more recently the government's Big Results Now programme that hopes to resolve constraints to delivering results in priority areas.[13]

Grounding this discussion in the theory of elites presented in Chapter 3, MPs are members of an elite who require the support of the winning coalition and the ruling party to retain their positions. As high-level corruption is often linked to political and economic elites, and is endemic, 'those who might be convicted are in a position to accuse others' (Tripp 2012:12). As the networks are fluid and changeable, and payoffs extend beyond the short term, this makes it very risky to identify past rent seeking that might have been illegal. This is compounded by the factionalist nature of political elites and increasing political competition.

The rhetoric around corruption has been prevalent since President Mkapa's first term when the 1996 Presidential Commission of Inquiry Against Corruption led by Joseph Warioba reported that corruption was rampant and named 70 people (Tripp 2012). No prosecutions followed, although an anti-corruption strategy was formed, and a unit was established to coordinate anti-corruption activities.[14] Despite the high-level corruption being identified as perpetrated by political leaders (Muganda 1997: 4), these initiatives were unable to hold those responsible to account; the absence of high-level prosecutions remains notable.

As discussed earlier, the EPA and the Richmond high-level corruption cases resulted in the establishment of special parliamentary committees. Both cases received extensive media attention and even played an active role in prompting the investigation. Although these cases were just two of many, high-level corruption arguably returned to the fore of public consciousness as a result.[15] However, the ability of the political and business elites to protect themselves is evident in the absence of convictions, as prominent politicians have lost their seats through corruption investigations but prosecutions have not resulted and businesspersons have also not been prosecuted (Anon 2007). This is especially notable in the Richmond case, which resulted in the resignation of the Prime Minister (BBC 2008), yet no convictions followed. Furthermore, these scandals have not affected the reputation of CCM (Mattes 2008).

---

cent in the three preceding presidential elections (Joint Donor Governance Working Group, December 2010 provisional analysis of the 2010 elections).

  13    For example, the Minister for Public Service Management in the President's Office.

  14    That is, the National Anti-Corruption Strategy and Action Plan and the Good Governance Co-ordination Unit.

  15    Other cases include IPTL (Independent Power Tanzania Limited), the British Aerospace radar and the Kiwira Coal Mine.

**Table 5.1    Types of stability-maintaining activities, levels of coordination and degrees of resource diversion**

| Type of activity | Level of coordination | Resource diversion | Example |
|---|---|---|---|
| CCM's explicit vote-mobilisation strategy of providing visible public goods country-wide | Centrally coordinated | This may divert provision from less visible, but goods that have important welfare benefits, in which case there is reduced allocative efficiency of public goods | Building primary schools, farm subsidies, conditional cash transfers |
| Returning favours from private sector actors through benefits | Centrally coordinated/ personalized | Revenue forgone; less competitive procurement practices; reduced allocative efficiency of public goods | Taxation benefits; contract acquisition; a favourable adjustment in the allocation of public goods |
| Local-level capture by politicians or local leaders providing (often visible) goods to villages or wards in an attempt to secure their position | Local-level strategy | May reduce allocative efficiency of public goods Often privately financed through with implications for the cost of competing in elections and for the incentives that local actors face to solve collective action problems | Visible: provision of water pumps to villages. Less visible: provision of maize to farmers |

*Source*: Author's analysis.

> [The press] helped to raise Richmond case and had an influential role in corruption fighting but after Richmond the media and business interests colluded to protect themselves, which equalled silence. (Interview with politician, CCM, Head of special committee, June 2009)

This activity, undertaken to ensure stability, involves rent seeking and has a cost of enforcement. It therefore diverts some resources away from the delivery of public services. It also possibly involves a reduction in the allocative efficiency of public expenditure if it diverts provision from less visible goods that are, however, no less important for the welfare of beneficiaries and may have been identified as priorities by the community.[16] This occurs in three forms. The first one is centrally

---

16    The interest is not in the occurrence of inefficiency, but rather in the degree of the efficiency loss that is conjectured to be inversely proportional to the degree of centralisation. While a crucial issue for exploration, we do not pursue this here; refer to the work of others,

coordinated, the second may be centrally coordinated or more personal, and the last one is most commonly a local-level strategy, as outlined in Table 5.1.

1. CCM's explicit vote mobilisation strategy of providing visible public goods country-wide, (such as building primary schools), diverting provision from less visible, but equally important, goods.
2. Returning favours from private-sector actors through benefits in the form of tax evasion, which represents lost revenue; contract acquisition; or a favourable adjustment in the allocation of public goods.
3. Local-level capture by politicians or local leaders providing (often visible) goods to villages or wards in an attempt to secure their position. This changes incentives for actors at the local level to find solutions for collective action problems because, if public goods are not maintained by the village, a politician may ultimately step in and deliver new infrastructure.

Despite the resulting reduced efficiency provision, this allows public services to be delivered, and personalisation and embeddedness provide knowledge and respect and therefore facilitate the fulfilment of designated roles (Evans et al. 1996, Kelsall et al. 2010). As voice increases and, similarly, the movement towards individual MPs pursuing their own interests, it could be argued that the ability of CCM to maintain an ideological hegemony will decline. This may provide a stronger check on the executive (Hyden 2010). Applying their model of rent management, Kelsall et al. (2013) characterised Tanzania as a mixed model, with characteristics of both 'centralised long-horizon rent management' as well as 'decentralized short-horizon rent management', based on the loose centralisation of rent seeking in CCM, the macro reforms that have centralised rents, as well as recent political liberalisation that provides an incentive for 'unproductive rent seeking and corruption' (Kelsall et al. 2013: 153).

The reality of politics in Tanzania is one of powerful interest groups serving well-established political settlements, and of votes being attained through the provision of public goods, often in the form of gifts to local communities. This has been compounded in recent years by the factionalist nature of political elites, and increasing political competition. Throughout, the politician's role is to maintain the systems of patronage and ensure state, donor and private sector resources are used to maintain their interests (Thornton and Meena 2010). This involves securing projects and investments for their own constituencies (a prime objective for all MPs), and also obtaining access to rents in various ways, which helps them access the resources required to consolidate or grow their political networks and following.

Both high-level and petty corruption is perceived as extensive, although the increase in media attention to corruption may have greatly increased expectations, along with perceptions of the prevalence of corruption, indicating an increase in the

including the Africa Power and Politics Programme (http://www.institutions-africa.org/), for more details.

demand for accountability by society. This increased awareness of corruption may actually be indicative of an improvement in the control of corruption, as increased awareness is generated and it becomes perceived as less socially acceptable.

## 5.3 Societal Accountability

This section analyses how civil society is placed within Tanzanian society, and in relation to the state. It considers its historical roots, and updates these with an analysis of contemporary accountability to society. Societal accountability is a concept that is understood at the local level, unlike governmental accountability (Kelsall et al. 2005). However, it is recognised that this aggregate concept masks the complex interplay and overlap between different institutions at the local level (Kelsall et al.2005).

There is a unique and complex relationship between the state and citizens in Tanzania at the local level. This creates an adverse context for forming a social contract. To build on examples discussed previously, Kelsall (2004) finds a lack of accountability of politicians; a lack of information; low capacity in councils; and corruption at the top level. How, then, does accountability to society work through civil society in contemporary Tanzania? It is analysed here in terms of the demand for and supply of accountability, and analysed through public access to information; civil-society influence on expenditure priorities; press freedom; and the budget process.

### Civil-society Organisations

Historically, the strength of the Tanzanian state has come at the expense of civil society: from the 1960s there were efforts to dissolve civil society and 'remould it in the image of the state itself' (Kiondo 1995: 110). Civil society was marginalised, by organisations being demobilised and absorbed into the state and the party, thus preventing any significant uprisings; this, in turn, aided the legitimacy of the party (Hyden 1994, Shivji 2006). Legislatively, this commenced with the 1954 Societies Ordinance, a colonial movement to ban people's organisations (Shivji 2006). Many civil-society organisations were co-opted into the state, becoming wings of the ruling party, and a policy of unspoken tolerance and non-interference was cultivated between the church/mosque and the state (Pinkney 1997). The party both marginalised and actively suppressed civil-society organisations (Barkan 1994, Hyden 1994, Mercer 1999), groups such as trade unions were seen as subordinate to the party (Berg-Schlosser and Siegler 1990), and there was an ambivalence, linked to low expectations, towards influencing national policy (Pinkney 1997). These things together produced an enabling environment for the incorporation or subordination of any organisations considered threats to the party, including the army and trade unions.

It was only when reforms took place from the late 1980s and (albeit weak) democracy emerged that the growth of civil society was encouraged. This resulted in a proliferation of organisations, including non-governmental organisations, which increased in number from 163 registered in 1990 to 224 in 1993 (Kiondo 1995). Shivji (2006) highlights that, declarations aside, civil-society actors are not politically neutral, because they are still trying to gain state power and influence. He notes two reasons why this is the case: 1) acts of government have an impact on their work and aims; and 2) the organisations are dealing with issues that arise at the interface between state and society, for example, workers' rights and issues of land ownership. Non-governmental organisations are central to the interface between the state and society, and are located firmly within Level B of the model of elites discussed in Chapter 3. They are therefore within the middle level of elites, although some more influential members also maintain roles and interests within other groups and sit within the fringes of Level A.

For society to demand accountability, a desire for political organisation is necessary. However, social action is not always within people's control (Kelsall 2004), particularly because the move to see the poor as a collective group has arisen from the top. This notion has been imposed on the poor through policy documents such as poverty reduction strategy papers. Concerted collective action requires strong collective identities, but the increasing diversification of livelihoods means social relations in Tanzania involve a range of crosscutting networks spanning a range of diverse economic and social commitments (Kelsall 2004).[17] Therefore, to take action against a village chairman may involve offending someone who is also within the same network as oneself. Direct reprisals are not necessarily an issue, but one's own economic and social interests may be threatened as a result of complex overlapping networks, and there is a desire not to close down options by causing offence to others. In negotiation situations, peasants are more likely to use exit than voice and therefore do not exercise their collective identities (Hyden 1980, Isaacman 1996).

In the mid-twentieth century in Tanzania, 'peasantization', and an upsurge in rural institution building and peasant political action were associated with homogeneous rural activities (Iliffe 1971). In the late twentieth century, this eroded, owing to a worsening of international conditions for agriculture and policies that weakened export agriculture in the 1970s, resulting in diversification. Social theories that stress the fragmentation of identities (for example, post-modernists, post-colonialists and post-structuralists), emphasise that each individual has a plurality of different identities (Kelsall 2004). This draws us away from the assumption frequently applied in orthodox economics, of a homogeneous actor with a predetermined utility function, and instead points to heterogeneous individuals facing different incentives.

---

17    Kelsall specifically studied Arumeru district in northern Tanzania, although this pattern is considered here to be generalisable to social relations countrywide.

As the weakness of collective action results in exit, the use of voice reduces (Iliffe 1971). The plurality of different identities and the dynamic nature of social relations, combined with the actions of the state to undermine any attempts towards collective organisation, ensure the maintenance of power by the incumbent elite.

> People are not citizens, as they are just told what to do – they are more like subjects. Access to information will not solve the accountability issue as people and civil society are sheepish and at the mercy of local officials who they don't want to offend. (Interview with senior researcher, June 2010)

Civil society has only a limited influence on public expenditure policy. This is partly a result of limited capacity in civil-society organisations, combined with constraints on their operation that limit their effectiveness. Studies on the impact of civil-society budget analysis depend on the public expenditure context. This includes i) opportunities relating to external factors, such as legal and institutional frameworks determining access to budget information, the presence and role played by international donor agencies, and overall level of literacy and interest in budget issues; ii) internal factors such as the leadership, technical capacity of budget groups and their communication/dissemination abilities; and iii) the networks that budget groups have established to allow them to influence policy (de Renzio 2007). These findings are borne out in Tanzania.

Openings for civil society to provide its views on the priorities for public expenditure are limited. The main annual forum is Poverty Policy Week, which usually takes place during October or November. The Public Expenditure Review (PER) Consultative Group used to be the main forum bringing in non-governmental groups, but this involved only a small minority of civil-society groups that were close to government and usually based in Dar es Salaam. Consultations held with the public are considered 'very limited' and to involve 'only a few constituencies', and the list of invitees to the annual PER consultation is limited and exclusionary (International Budget Partnership 2007: 60): 'there is no formal mechanism for pre- and post-budget consultation between government and farmers' representatives, public interest groups or labour unions' (Naschold and Fozzard 2002: 48). Meetings of the PER macro and main groups used to take place throughout the year and to have limited civil-society participation; however, since around 2007, they have not been meeting, largely because of senior staff changes in the Ministry of Finance and Economic Affairs. A PER champions group was formed in 2012 with the aim of reviving the PER.[18]

Next, we consider public access to information, and its relation to societal accountability followed by a discussion of accountability in the budget process.

---

18    Rather than it being sector focused, like the old PER, it is issue focused and, at the time of writing, studies are planned for tax exemptions, the private sector, a public expenditure tracking study for selected local government, and agricultural subsidies.

*The Media and Access to Information*

As Chapter 2 discussed, the media is an important conduit for demanding vertical accountability. In Tanzania, the media has proliferated during the past decade and ownership has broadened. Previously, all newspapers and radio were owned by government, whereas there are now more than 18 daily newspapers and 60 radio stations (African Media Barometer 2010). Although ownership is more diverse, the media remains co-opted into elite groups through pervasive connections with the state class, through either ownership linkages or funding.

Since 1980, Tanzania's rating of civil liberties, including freedom of expression, has moved from un-free to partially free and the country's rating for press freedom has remained fairly constant since 2001 (Freedom House 2009a). Legislatively, freedom is limited, because the president appoints the leadership of the Tanzania Communication Regulatory Authority. There are also a number of laws still in place that limit freedom of expression, for example, the Public Services Act (1962), the Newspaper Act (1976), the Penal Code (1945, revised 2002), the National Security Act (1970) and the Public Leadership Code of Ethics Act (1995) (African Media Barometer 2010).

Government interference in the media prevails, and attacks on the media and journalists continue (Freedom House 2009b, 2012). Intimidation of journalists is most commonly carried out indirectly through the withdrawal of advertising revenue, but it can also involve more violent and personal attacks:

> Violence is still carried out and Mwanhalisi [the vocal weekly investigative paper] has been the victim of acid attacks and police searches and when the Bank of Tanzania Twin Towers [corruption scandal] was revealed by the Sunday Citizen, advertising was withdrawn. This is a disaster, as newspapers need advertising revenue to survive. (Interview with editor of a leading newspaper, July 2009)

Furthermore, since 2008, there have been suspensions of newspapers: *Mwanahalisi* was suspended in 2008 and *Kulikoni* in 2010. Media freedom legislation remains unpassed despite extensive advocacy efforts. In 2011 the managing editor and a staff member of *Tanzania Daima* were charged with incitement after an article about the misuse of police (Freedom House 2012).

> There are occasional requests not to publish via requests to delay or hold stories, always done very politely by an mzee [an elderly gentleman] making it difficult to refuse. Some people give in to this. (Interview with editor of a leading newspaper, July 2009)

> As we have seen, the proliferation of media outlets is linked to politics, with politicians often buying newspapers or radio stations. This political ownership of the media has the potential to increase the availability of information, the first stage in increasing accountability, but also risks being a constraint on truth and

democracy if there is no maintenance of quality or standards. It is estimated that the government controls approximately two-thirds of the media. (Interview with CCM politician and head of special committee, June 2009)

[The] media is ruling the country today ... however, no-one corrects what is reported on. Newspapers have too much power. There is total freedom of the media in the current regime and it shapes the direction of politics and people criticise Kikwete for giving too much freedom to media. (Interview with CCM politician, and ex-cabinet minister, June 2009)

The public's access to information is not legally established. While the constitution in Article 18 (amended in the 14th amendment of 2005) provides for freedom of access to information, this is not enshrined in a law. A Freedom of Information Bill has been under debate since it was gazetted in 2006. It has not been passed as law because of on-going discussions around accessing 'restricted' and 'classified' government information.[19]

Public access to fiscal information has improved 'through the dissemination of its reports on the national websites, and in government gazettes and local newspapers' (URT 2010: 21). This information is released in the media, and some is available only on the government website, so access by the public to such information remains limited. Understanding of the information requires the intervention of non-state actors, who can present and communicate such data in an appropriate manner. Routine work by non-governmental organisations has included lobbying government on issues of concern in public expenditure, and simplifying information, for example, audit reports and the popular guides to the poverty reduction strategy and poverty monitoring (Rajani 2007).

Information on, for example, resources for primary service providers, such as schools and health centres, is not provided (Public Financial Management Working Group 2009).[20] Such data are perhaps the most important for domestic accountability in the context of poverty reduction, as they would allow the public to demand accountability: 'Information on resources received by front line service delivery units is mostly lacking. Special surveys were undertaken within the last three years, but their results and methodologies used have not been published' (2009: 37). Similarly, there are no routine data provided on service delivery units, and special surveys are often not released, owing to disagreement over the results. This was the case for a 2004 Public Expenditure Tracking Survey (PETS) in

---

19    The draft bill presented to parliament in 2007 classified cabinet papers as secret. This was opposed by a coalition of civil-society organisations who presented government and parliament with an alternative bill (International Budget Partnership 2007, African Media Barometer 2010).

20    This is rated under Public Expenditure Framework Accountability Indicator PI-23: Availability of information on resources received by service delivery units. Tanzania scored a C in 2006 and a D in 2009 (URT 2010).

education, which found that less than half of the resources were released to their final intended destinations; this is further confirmed by personal communications:[21]

> [We found in one village] 75 per cent of [the] budgeted capitation grant [was] never reaching primary schools, not even reaching the district! (Personal communication with researcher, July 2010)

Among the weaknesses in the availability of information to the public is the fact that contract awards are not always complete and that budget execution reports and final accounts do not provide information broken down by ministries, departments and agencies, and therefore it is not possible to track the implementation of the budget. There is no functional classification of the budget that follows international standards, and information provided on the development budget is limited, which limits the financial information available.[22]

Two sequential studies evaluated the access the public has to information by placing requests with government and monitoring the results (Ally 2007; HakiElimu 2005). These found that access to information in Tanzania was poor, with approximately one-third of requests receiving responses. It is still challenging for citizens to access information on the budget (International Budget Partnership 2007: 103), with the main factors in this being 'bureaucratic culture, social relationships, and attitudes and motivations of requestees' (Ally 2007: iii).

## 5.4 Accountability and Public Financial Management

Public financial management reforms have been ongoing since the late 1990s, and are coordinated under the umbrella of the Public Financial Management Reform Programme that includes budget management, treasury management and accounting, procurement, information technology services, payroll, and external audit. The next section reviews progress in reforms that relate to accountability and budget implementation, procurement and audit.

---

21     The 2004 report was never released by government. However, a more recent education sector PETS found much lower levels of leakage: 9 per cent in primary education and 8 per cent in secondary education. The greatest problem noted was variation between councils: while some councils received less than 50 per cent of their budgeted amounts, others received 30 per cent more (Claussen and Assad 2010).

22     Development of the functional classification has been in progress since 2001, with much pressure from international agencies, but has yet to be implemented. Resistance to increased transparency of the budget may be encouraged by those interests that benefit from patronage payments.

*Budget Implementation, Procurement and Audit*

In the context of clientelism, the budget is a potential source of rents and therefore it is important to understand how the budget is implemented, including reallocations during the year and the audit process. The limited influence of civil society on the budget process, and challenges around the transparency of information have been discussed. This will now be complemented by the consideration of budget implementation, the point at which influence can be determined given the often weak correspondence between policy and practice.

The cash budgeting reforms and the Public Financial Management Reform Programme have increased the centralised control of rents, notably through the centralised payment system. However, a number of difficulties are experienced in implementing the budget as passed by parliament. These difficulties all offer opportunities for rent seeking. Cash budgeting was introduced in 1997 in response to an IMF recommendation to deal with the fiscal crisis. While it has achieved that aim, it has also led to delays in the purchase of goods and services and increasing suppliers' arrears, because funds are often not released in equal tranches throughout the year.[23]

The Public Financial Management Reform Programme has coordinated a range of expenditure management improvements including accounting and audit and a centralised payment system. These can be considered to be major improvements, which have also centralised the control of rents, although a lack of control over how funds are spent by agencies persists, with the result being waste and inefficiency (Kelsall et al. 2013). The implementation of the programme has also experienced a number of challenges and delays, which could be expected for extensive reforms that directly challenge the organisation and control of rents. These characteristics are discussed in more detail below.

A further area of inefficiency, limited information and therefore scope for rent seeking, is payroll. Where controls are insufficiently strong, arrears are often accrued and more frequent reconciliation is needed (Public Financial Management Working Group, Tanzania PEFA 2010). Budget reallocations during the year present an interesting case to analyse how budget implementation presents opportunities for rent seeking.

There are extensive reallocations both across and within spending agencies (or votes) within the fiscal year (Public Financial Management Working Group 2009), calling into question the credibility of the budget approved by parliament. In 2006/07, reallocations amounted to 14 per cent of expenditure but this was reduced to 5 per

---

23    The cash budget limited aggregate expenditure in a month to average revenue (domestic plus external) in the previous three months (Ngowi 2005). The development budget, in particular, typically experiences problems in implementation as a result of contract delays and changes during the budget year.

cent in 2007/08.[24] The process for a reallocation is that a form provided by Ministry of Finance and Economic Affairs has to be completed by the ministry, department or agency and submitted to the commissioner for the budget, who provides preliminary approval, followed by sign off by the paymaster general (namely, the Permanent Secretary, Ministry of Finance and Economic Affairs). Warrants applied during the year are compiled retrospectively into books, and submitted to parliament for *ex-post* approval halfway through the year, and at the end of the year. There have been delays in passing the bills in the past, however, one case being the Supplementary Bill for 2003/04, which was gazetted only in January 2007.

In addition to delays, there are other weaknesses with this process in terms of the transparency of the budget. First, while the budget is presented to parliament by line item, reallocation warrants are detailed only by sub-vote (areas of focus contributing to a programme), making comparison with the original budget impossible. Second, as this analysis considers expenditure only by broad category, other hidden priorities and patronage payments that may be on budget and planned in the budget-preparation process are masked. An example of this is payments that are worked into contracts for the procurement of works or services. Consequently, reallocations are often passed with inadequate information to allow a full understanding of the adjustments, providing scope for wastage and inefficiency.

Procurement accounts for around 70 per cent of total government expenditure, and the level of compliance with the 2004 Public Procurement Act has risen in recent years. During 2007/08, procurement audits undertaken by the Public Procurement Regulatory Authority found an average level of compliance of 43 per cent overall (URT 2008b), which had increased to 65 per cent in 2011 (URT 2012b).[25] This average masks a huge variance, however: assessed compliance varied between 73 per cent (the Tanzania Ports Authority) and 7 per cent (Tanzania Library Services) in 2008. A general weakness in the procurement process is the lack of publication of information on contract awards to the public, with only 66 per cent of open tenders advertised (URT 2008b).

The audit process has been a focus of successful efforts to increase capacity during the past 20 years, through the Public Financial Management Reform Programme supported by the Swedish government and other projects such as the Accountability, Transparency and Integrity Project (World Bank 2012, Robinson 2010). There are still calls for further improvement, however, and, while it covers central and local government and parastatal enterprises in part, the audit is constrained by the extent to which it can obtain information from districts. Therefore, the parliamentary Local Authority Accounts Committee plays an important role in supporting the central audit function, highlighting cases of fund misuse and requesting a special audit to follow up.

---

24    Author's calculations, based on data from Ministry of Finance and Economic Affairs, reallocation warrants, and the International Monetary Fund.

25    The indicators were revised between the two assessments so, while a trend improvement is clear, commenting on the scale of the change could be misleading.

The controller and auditor general can't investigate [all local accounts] as the distance makes it difficult. They [the auditors] need documents from districts and when [the districts] don't submit this leads to delays and the cases have to be dropped. (Interview with opposition politician, chair of Local Authority Accounts Committee, June 2009)

The independence of the National Audit Office was increased in the new Audit Act gazetted in September 2008, which allows the agency to recruit and dismiss its own staff and to determine their salaries. It also provides for a budget that no longer requires the approval of the Ministry of Finance and Economic Affairs. This independence is, however, limited by the fact that the controller and auditor general is a presidential appointee, and therefore must be aligned with the president in order to achieve the post. That said, even if the position were fully independent and the external audit had full coverage, external audits would not necessarily be able to capture all patronage payments, because these can still effectively be made within a robust budget process.

The final stage in the budget-implementation process is the resolution of audit queries. This is a weak process, with an absence of systematic follow-up by ministries, departments and agencies, and often delayed responses by the Ministry of Finance and Economic Affairs and the Parliamentary Accounts Committee. The follow-up of queries commences with a review of the audit report by the Parliamentary Accounts Committee and hearings held with accounting officers, which frequently highlight inconsistencies and weaknesses in the audit process (Public Financial Management Working Group 2009). Given the limited capacity of the Parliamentary Accounts Committee, its comments on the audit report routinely take more than one year to issue, following which, the Ministry of Finance and Economic Affairs issues a report requiring further action from ministries, departments and agencies, although there is no evidence of implementation of this (Public Financial Management Working Group 2009).

The power of parliament in terms of budget and public financial management issues is significantly less than that of the executive and, more specifically, than that of a small group of senior civil servants who influence the executive (concentrated in the Ministry of Finance and Economic Affairs, and the State House). A small sub-group is actively involved in the policy formulation stage and has the power to preside over the entire budget-preparation process, concentrated in the President's Office and the Ministry of Finance and Economic Affairs. This small group presides over the details of the budget, and the parliament and the wider civil service have little influence.[26] Mmari et al. (2005: ix) confirm that 'the Executive has a dominant role in setting the budget and is subject only to a rather

---

26    This is based on the author's direct experience of working on the preparation of the budget in the Ministry of Finance and of following the budget approval process through parliament, combined with secondary sources (Cooksey 2011, Mmari et al. 2005, Policy Forum 2009a).

formalistic scrutiny and oversight by Parliament'. They also find that, within the executive, it is a small sub-group that dominates, comprising 'the President and a small group of senior ministers' (Mmari et al. 2005: ix).

## 5.5 Summary: The State and Society in Tanzania

Tanzania's success has lain in its ability to ensure stability through rent redistribution, but this has been accompanied by a relatively weak state that has weakened further since the 1990s. The degree of state centralisation has varied during different periods of history: in earlier periods, the state was highly centralised whereas, more recently, it has become less so. Historically, society in Tanzania was relatively homogenous, allowing the ruling party to achieve inclusivity with little factional competition, which required only a limited redistribution of rents (Khan and Gray 2006). Since the mid-1990s the core of elites has become more fragmented, with different groups functioning through their separate clientelistic networks. Although the democratic system has become more open, and checks and balances have increased, the ruling party continues to dominate and there is increasing co-optation of different groups into elite networks. There has actually been a consolidation of parties, and a reduction in political choice (Beck et al. 2001, World Bank database of political institutions[27]), with the party fulfilling the function of a coercive instrument of the state.

Recently, political stability and patterns of rent seeking have begun to change, with factors including vocal MPs becoming more prominent, the emergence of a credible opposition party, an increased regionalism in politics, and reduced state institutional capacity all playing a role. Stability has, however, been ensured, and the inclusiveness of CCM has successfully kept dissenting influences mainly within the party, and has helped to maintain its legitimacy. The leadership has been able to maintain control, since the factions in the centre that are in competition with one another are not particularly strong, and a certain fluidity allows some reshuffling across these internal factions. Domestic accountability is characterised by this absence of the effective central coordination of rent seeking.

The party elite represents the interface between the leadership and society, as it is *influenced by* as well as *influencing* society. Applying the interpretation of Wright Mills's model of elites (Figure 3.1, Chapter 3), the party and the leadership are influenced by the societal structures of power and legitimacy. Furthermore, the state is often perceived to be a homogenous entity, whereas we have seen that the complex realities of different interests and competing factions are, in fact, paramount. The effectiveness of the leadership depends on the balance between the competing factions, and relates to the dominant faction's ability to control power. Our brief discussion of Kikwete's presidency has highlighted the factional nature of the inner core of elites: continual contestation results in fluidity as actors move

---

27    http://go.worldbank.org/2EAGGLRZ40.

between factions and positions, within a network where coalitions are protecting particular interests. The relational accountability framework acknowledges the key role played by elites or certain interest groups, to which the government is required to make patronage payments in order to keep receiving their support. This ensures stability and the retention of power by the incumbent party. This has developed the relationship between political leaders and business leaders as political competition has increased. CCM has also successfully co-opted businesses, in such a way that party endorsement facilitates business establishment and operation, and, in turn, provides rents for the party.

Powerful interest groups within the executive with close ties to business have redistributed resources to maintain the support of elites for the ruling party. Through a strategy of CCM to mobilise votes, this reduces the allocative efficiency of public expenditure in several ways: by providing visible public goods; by returning favours from private sector actors through benefits (such as through evasion of taxation, which represents lost revenue); by contract acquisition; by an adjustment in the allocation of public goods; or by local level capture by politicians and local leaders providing goods to villages or wards.

Electoral accountability to the population (and the answerability of those elected) are weak in Tanzania, as there is a lack of real policy choices for the electorate. The Western model of accountability, on which the state creation model is based, is not applicable here. Political stability is maintained through patron–client networks as politicians visibly deliver public goods to ensure votes, in explicit support of CCM's strategies. Furthermore, stability is supported at the local level by resource capture and clientelistic distribution that maintains individuals in their positions of power. This sits within the realm of relational accountability, rather than formal and contractual procedural accountability. The high degree of political stability points to payoffs within CCM that are sufficient to contain factional competition (Khan and Gray 2006).

This chapter has considered the nature of societal accountability in sociopolitical terms, by assessing the availability of information to the public as a stage in accountability, the influence on policy, and the implementation of the budget. The strong arm of the party, and the domination of the country by the same elite caucus for 50 years, has come at the expense of civil society, which has been co-opted and restrained to allow the party to maintain power. This supports Gramsci's (1971: 253) notion of 'political society', where the state and civil society are intertwined, and both rule and govern. Many of the non-governmental organisations engaged in dialogue with the executive have been co-opted, and are themselves members of elites. The discussion above has highlighted the executive's continued dominance in policy formulation and implementation, and its responsiveness to the demands of clientelistic networks. Civil-society influence on expenditure priorities is limited, and openings for civil society to provide its views on priorities for public expenditure are few, because consultations include only a limited circle of the elite who have close ties with the government. There has certainly been an expansion in the number of newspapers, particularly those owned by politicians, meaning the media has become increasingly co-opted into the state class.

Public financial management reforms have been ongoing since the late 1990s, and substantial progress has been made in treasury management, procurement, information technology services and external audit: reforms that have centralised the control of rent payments (Kelsall et al. 2013). The implementation of the reform programme also has experienced a number of challenges and delays, as could be expected for extensive reforms which directly challenge the organisation and control of rents. Areas of inefficiency persist, including payroll, cash management, budget reallocations during the year (presenting opportunities for rent seeking), limited information flows between central and local government, and poor follow-up of audit queries. The implementation of the budget is key. Rather than the policy setting process being important, the real influence happens during the policy implementation process, which is when policy is actually determined (Kjær and Therkildsen 2013).

In Tanzania, there is a complex and established web of relational accountability relationships, and a broad circle of trust is actively maintained through consideration of the extended family, and of the overlap between the private and the public domains. These broader influences of relational accountability are more relevant than the conventional assessment of a narrow procedural accountability relationship that exists, for example, solely between elected officials and civil society, and which is centred on a social contract. Chapter 6 will build on this understanding of how procedural and relational accountability interact in the sociopolitical environment, through an analysis of the two types of accountability within the context of foreign aid.

# Chapter 6

# The Interaction between Procedural and Relational Accountability: Foreign Aid in Tanzania

## 6.1 Introduction

This chapter analyses foreign aid in Tanzania by applying the theory discussed in earlier chapters, in particular the accountability framework articulated in Chapter 3. In doing so, we move towards a picture of aid that is within the relational level of the theoretical framework.

We take it as a given that aid is greater than the sum of financial flows and associated conditionalities, and see it as a pattern of social relations shaped by context and history. We review the recent history of aid provision to Tanzania in the context of foreign aid relations, outlining the scale of aid and analysing of the impact of aid on public finances. We focus particularly on general budget support (GBS), as this is the largest aid modality in Tanzania in terms of volume of funds and number of donors, where donors jointly negotiate with the government. GBS therefore provides an important platform for considering how relational and procedural accountability interact. We consider the models of conditionality presented in Chapter 4, extending this analysis to explore the power relations and credibility issues associated with the interactions between donors and the government.

We analyse donor-government relations through the lenses of procedural and relational accountability, the foreign policy context, and the motivations of successive Tanzanian governments and donors in the international aid environment. We consider how the increased use of formal frameworks that are procedural in nature and structure require relational characteristics (such as negotiation and manoeuvring) in their implementation. This reflects the foreign policy objectives of donors, often implicitly, and plays a key part in negotiations around the delivery of aid. Our examination of aid management provides insights into the tensions between procedural accountability and relational accountability. The relational notion of accountability places foreign aid in the context of the wider system, considering how it is influenced by domestic politics, building on the state and society analysis in Chapter 5. We also analyse conditionality in Tanzania and describe the changing relationship with donors over different periods of Tanzania's recent history.

## 6.2 How General Budget Support Emerged and what it Meant for Aid Relations

Having reviewed the sociopolitical context in Tanzania and analysed the nature of accountability, we can now ask how the patterns of aid, and specifically GBS, have influenced accountability relationships. This section considers different types of aid in the context of other sources of revenue in Tanzania. In particular, we discuss the mechanisms for the delivery of aid and the agreements and conditionalities underlying GBS.

Aid inflows have played a key role in both fiscal sustainability and the delivery of public services in Tanzania; it is through the latter that the population can feel the direct impact of aid. During the 2000s, total aid inflows (grants plus loans) as a percentage of government expenditure rose fairly rapidly, from 29 per cent in 2000/01 to 42 per cent in 2007/08. At the time, Tanzania was one of the largest recipients of aid in sub-Saharan Africa (GBS Donors 2007, Government of Tanzania 2008). The particularly sharp increase until 2003/04 (see Figure 6.1) is due to new donors disbursing GBS and therefore joining the group. At its peak, this saw membership rise to 14 donors: 11 bilateral donors and three multilateral donors.[1] The move towards GBS was sustained until 2007, although around a fluctuating trend.

The share of Tanzania's budget that aid makes up has been maintained, funding almost one third of total expenditure. However, the share of grants within this has declined: in 2005/06 grants amounted to 24 per cent of total expenditure, but by 2010/11 grants financed only 17 per cent of total expenditure, a fall of 30 per cent (IMF 2009, 2013).

Comparing aid to domestic revenue collections, Figure 6.1 shows tax revenue as being over four times greater than GBS. Tax financed an average of 58 per cent of total expenditure, whereas GBS financed an average of 15 per cent. It is interesting to note that almost half of Tanzania's tax revenue is financed by large companies through the Large Taxpayer Department. Therkildsen and Bourgouin have pointed to the potential influence arising from this 'if power follows money' (Therkildsen and Bourgouin, 2012: 38).

Development expenditure is the proxy for project inflows as, while it includes a small domestically financed component financed by taxation, such as matching grants or counterpart funding (which varies by project), it is dominated by externally financed projects. These comprised between 62 and 81 per cent of all

---

1    Switzerland and the Netherlands stopped providing GBS in 2011. In 2012 there were a total of 12 donors. Bilateral donors included Canada, Denmark, Finland, Germany, Ireland, Japan, Norway, Sweden, United Kingdom. Multilateral donors included the European Commission, the World Bank, and the African Development Bank.

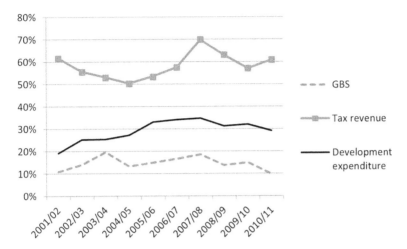

**Figure 6.1** **Tax revenue and GBS as a percentage of total expenditure**

*Source:* Ministry of Finance data

development expenditure during the decade.[2] This includes basket funding support which we now compare to GBS.

Figure 6.2 shows the rate of growth of GBS, tax revenue and total expenditure. The slower growth of GBS, and its decline in recent years, can be seen clearly.

It is useful to compare levels of GBS to funding from other modalities were donors are jointly organised. In 2011/12, USD 562 million was committed as GBS, whereas total donor basket fund support amounted to USD 430 million (URT 2013). The latter comprises different donor groups, organised by sector.[3] Table 6.1 shows donor disbursements to the main sector basket funds for 2010/11 and 2011/12. The health sector received the largest amount of funds in both years (even when we exclude HIV/AIDS, a separate and much smaller fund). The Water Sector Development Programme is another large sector programme, amounting to USD 1.2 billion between 2011 and 2014. Of this, USD 588 million of this was financed by donors from 2006/7 to 2014, with the remainder being financed by the Tanzanian government.

---

2 This is symptomatic of a weakness in the budget classification system, as such a division is misleading and the development and recurrent budget ideally should be fully integrated.

3 Disbursements through baskets during 2011/12 were particularly low at USD 292m due to underperformance of a number of basket funds.

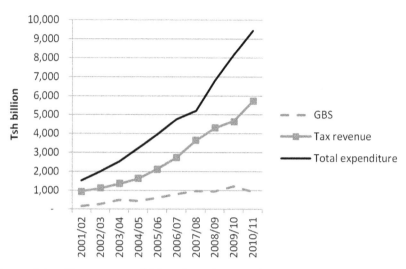

**Figure 6.2    Tax revenue, GBS and total expenditure, Tsh billions**
*Source:* Ministry of Finance data

**Table 6.1    Donor disbursements through major sector basket funds, USD millions**

|  | 2010/11 | 2011/12 | Average |
|---|---|---|---|
| Health (excluding HIV/AIDS) | 87.7 | 103.5 | 95.6 |
| Agriculture | 68.3 | 59.5 | 63.9 |
| Local government | 62.6 | 35.8 | 49.2 |
| Water | 71.6 | 9.7 | 40.6 |
| Education (secondary and primary) | 44.8 | 0.7 | 22.7 |

*Source*: compiled from URT (2013)

We have seen how GBS compares to other forms of revenue and therefore its relative importance to the government budget. Along with the indirect support to political reform provided by GBS, Table 6.2 outlines other donor funded initiatives that are related to accountability. The largest reform programmes: good governance and public sector reforms. Civil society was supported by the largest number of donors, followed by elections and democracy initiatives. The initiative with the greatest amount of financing in this area was the Deepening Democracy Programme, a basket fund coordinated by UNDP that ran from 2007 to 2010. Nine donors contributed USD17.7 million to this programme (Tripp 2012). In her analysis of donor support to institutions of accountability Tripp notes how donor funding through GBS, support for the removal of the development levy

**Table 6.2     Direct donor support to political reform, 2000–2010**

| Area of support | USD million | Donor |
|---|---|---|
| Good governance | 109.2 | World Bank, AfDF, UK, Denmark, Germany, The Netherlands, Norway |
| Public sector reform | 95.9 | World Bank, UK,, The Netherlands |
| Civil society | 84.7 | Norway, Finland, US, Germany, The Netherlands, Ireland, Switzerland, Canada, Austria, UNICEF, Sweden, New Zealand |
| Legal reform | 55.4 | World Bank, Canada, Denmark |
| Elections, voter registry | 41.7 | UK, Sweden Norway, Ireland, The Netherlands, EC, Denmark, Belgium, Canada, Italy, Spain |
| Advocacy: children's rights | 35.9 | UNICEF, US, Norway, The Netherlands |
| Democracy and civic education | 34.1 | Denmark, EC, Canada, UK, Norway, Sweden, The Netherlands, UNDP, Switzerland, Finland, Ireland |
| Advocacy: gender | 32.0 | Sweden, The Netherlands, Norway, UK, Germany, Switzerland, Belgium |
| Local government reform | 30.7 | UK, Ireland, Finland, Germany, Sweden, UNICEF |
| Human rights | 27.3 | Sweden, Denmark, UK, Finland, Germany, EC, Norway, Ireland |
| Media | 18.8 | Sweden, Switzerland, Norway |
| Peace | 2.2 | UNDP, Norway, Sweden |

*Source*: Tripp 2012: 4 using data from AidData
This table is reproduced here by permission of UNU-WIDER, who commissioned the original research and holds copyright thereon.

and support for large infrastructure companies has undermined procedural accountability (Tripp 2012).

   Along with changes in the financing through GBS, the nature of the agreements between donors and government have also evolved, increasing the transaction costs for government to manage GBS.

*Aid Agreements and Transaction Costs*

Turning to the impact of the structure of aid on transaction costs in Tanzania, we argue that the increase in procedural accountability, as the international aid environment becomes more formalised, is associated with increased transaction costs. As discussed in Chapter 4, Kanbur (2000) considers dependency in terms the demands that aid places on the time of the recipient government's civil servants and diverts from domestic consensus building and debate.

The Tanzanian government's stated preference for funds to be channelled through the budget-support mechanism has the potential to reduce transaction costs for the Ministry of Finance and Economic Affairs.[4] It has also encouraged more formal working practices for the GBS group of donors and the adoption of 'quiet times' to contain transaction costs. There is, however, a higher administrative burden, largely due to more extensive dialogue with donors resulting from their deeper involvement in the reform processes.

The move towards GBS involves a shift in power from line ministries to the Ministry of Finance, as aid is centralised. Donor funded projects provide direct control to the overseeing and implementing agencies and direct access to donors provides the possibility to negotiate funding and support to preferred initiatives. GBS removes this control as the Ministry of Finance determines how financing should be allocated. There is, however, no clear evidence that this has happened to the degree possible as 'there remain too many projects and too many common basket funds, working off budget, undermining ownership and generating transaction costs' (Booth et al. 2005: 143). Furthermore, the recent trend for donors to reduce their GBS allocations indicates some rebalancing back towards sector ministries, although predominantly in the form of sector budget support rather than traditional projects.

The reality on the ground is that a large amount of human resources are permanently dedicated to interacting with donors. Tasks include negotiations, scheduled reviews, *ad hoc* meetings, preparation of data and monitoring and reporting on progress in a wide range of reform areas. A recent report found that Tanzania provided 2,400 quarterly reports to donors in 2007 (Tandon 2008).[5] The government is overloaded with a large number of different reform programmes, which Therkildsen (2000: 64) terms 'reformitis', characterised by duplication, lack of coordination and excessive reporting requirements that impede effective service improvements.

Applying the analysis from Chapter 5, it is unlikely that, in the absence of these reporting demands, there would be a significant increase in the effectiveness and efficiency of service delivery by the public sector. The clientelistic nature of society requires that resources are allocated not simply in the most efficient manner, but also in a way that both enables payoffs to maintain local level capture, as local leaders and politicians seek to retain power, as well as to provide visible public goods to support Chama Cha Mapinduzi's (CCM's) re-election, as we saw in Chapter 5 (Kjær and Therkildsen 2013, Therkildsen and Bourgouin 2012).

---

4    Henceforth referred to as the Ministry of Finance.

5    It is unclear whether all of these are reports requested by donors as a conditionality or monitoring requirement, or whether the figure includes government reports that are supplied to donors.

### 6.3  The Hidden Agendas of Donors and Government: Foreign Policy and Aid

This section discusses Tanzania's foreign policy, building on the discussion in Chapter 5, and briefly outlines the foreign policy of its donors, with a focus on the GBS group. We then bring together these two influences in a discussion of power, considering donors in the Tanzanian context and the extent of their direct and indirect influence on policy.

*Tanzania's Foreign Policy*

The 1980s saw aid beginning to return to Tanzania, after relations with most foreign governments (notably excluding China) had weakened as a result of Nyerere's strongly nationalist and independent stance. After the collapse of communism in Eastern Europe, there was increasing focus and accompanying pressure from donors on democratisation and accountability in Africa, with aid to Tanzania accompanied by discussions of how democracy could be introduced. This mirrored the domestic debate and demands for democratisation (Shivji 2006), ahead of the 1992 move towards multiparty democracy. As we saw in Chapter 5, the introduction of democracy was important in legitimising CCM. The move towards democracy was therefore motivated by a domestic need for political legitimacy and supported by external pressures.

The return of aid should not be interpreted as extending to a positive relationship between donors and the Tanzanian government; rather, as Helleiner (2002: 251) notes, the aid relationship was 'in a perilous state'. Mkapa's first term as president commenced in 1995 in the context of a lack of trust between donors and the government. This was based on perceptions of poor administration, corruption, lack of democracy, budget mismanagement and the 'prickly' personality of the finance minister Helleiner 2002: 251). This environment was soon to change. Mkapa's second term (until 2005) saw a stronger pursuit of neoliberalism, the promotion of globalisation (*utandawazi*) and entrepreneurship (*ujasiriamali*), and a close allegiance between donors and government on the one hand, and the political elite and the business elite on the other. These allegiances capture the importance of the characteristics of relational accountability, including personal and informal networks of support.

A fiscal crisis and donor concern about the management of fiscal policy resulted in the freezing of aid in the mid-1990s. With support from a small group of donors, led by the Danish government, an independent group was formed to review the aid situation and to act as a mediator (Harrison and Mulley 2007). The resulting Helleiner Report of 1995 (Helleiner et al. 2002) identified government capacity as the key constraint and pointed to the need to improve partnerships and develop greater local ownership and trust between the government and donors – a 'liberal project of state-making' where reliance replaces coercion (Gould 2005: 6). From this point onwards, the emphasis has been on the embedding of an explicit performance-focused relationship based on a transparent monitoring and evaluation framework (Gore 2000). This is characteristic of a rise in procedural accountability, seen in the increasingly formalised approach of donors.

The 1995 Helleiner Report has been cited as a showcase for donor-government relations and a movement towards a more genuine dialogue between the government and donors (Helleiner 2002). However, Mkapa 'saw the economy through the eyes of the IMF [International Monetary Fund] or World Bank', and increasingly sought legitimacy from donors rather than from the people (Shivji 2006: 11). We must therefore tell the story from the perspective of relational accountability, to question what is genuine dialogue and what is happening below the surface.

President Mkapa's approach was not as simple as an endorsement of neoliberalism. Rather, the government is fully aware of the external face it must present in order to obtain foreign aid, and real legitimacy is sought from domestic, not international, sources. The issue is the extent to which the government, and specifically the president, can be perceived as seeking legitimacy from donors and still be accepted domestically. Mkapa was skilled at managing both, and he built his domestic legitimacy on reformist policies which supported the private sector; in turn, the influential middle classes experienced the gains of economic growth. Therefore, in the context of the accountability framework, he fostered procedural accountability through his compliance with the policies of donors but also, in co-opting the private sector, he facilitated the redistribution of resources necessary to buy and maintain support for the ruling party, in the spirit of relational accountability.

The close relationship fostered between donors and government under Mkapa's second term is seen by some as a 'conditionality of objectives' rather than a natural consensus (Harrison and Mulley 2007: 9). This reflects the perspective that a game was being played and the Tanzanian government was facilitating the emergence of an allegiance with donors. While there is a degree of mutual dependency (Harrison 2001) in terms of a coincidence of interests to disburse aid, overall there is a pulling in different directions in pursuit of opposing interests in the implementation of many major reforms.

To apply the analogy of Kelsall (2002: 597), an external consensus with donors is built through a 'shop-window' display which adopts the language of good governance. However, the rooms where the government's position is actually formed are 'smoke-filled', so as to capture complex interests involving relationships between the state and wider society, the extended family and the public-private interface. We consider the apparent disappearance of the dichotomy between the interests of donors and government between 2000 and 2005 to be an illusion based on a small elite group in government becoming apt at interacting with donors to reap their own gains, whether directly or indirectly. Nevertheless, this elite still has to maintain its circle of trust and to 'feed its children', and look after their extended family or those they wish to influence.[6]

---

6    Kelsall (2008) draws on Schatzberg's (2002) analogy with food and children, and applied it to Tanzanian society.

The approach of Mkapa's two terms differs from that of Kikwete, whose re-domesticisation has involved a retreat from the sphere of the budget-support donors and an increasingly selective international policy. This has enabled more active pursuit of a domestic agenda, allowing closer attention to domestic coalitions, which in turn has had an impact on the relationship with GBS donors. The increasing global influence of China, the increasing availability of finance from other donors without dialogue and conditionalities attached, and expectations of future hydrocarbon revenues (triggering increased non-concessional private sector financing) have had an effect on the response of the Tanzanian government to GBS donors. The government has retreated from its close relationship with budget-support donors, and instances of conflict (discussed further below) have eroded trust between the two groups.

*Donors' Foreign Policy*

While the higher-level political interests discussed in Chapter 4 are implicitly connected to aid (as aid is related to influence) the explicit aim of foreign aid among the group of GBS donors is to pursue policy objectives in line with both poverty reduction and the international aid agenda. In doing so, they are ensuring the disbursement of increasing amounts of aid in a harmonised manner (OECD 2008). This agenda has involved a shift towards a more formalised aid relationship, located within the procedural levels of Williamson's hierarchy and which takes no account of the higher-level influences of relational accountability. We see, however, relational accountability characteristics being used in the implementation of aid agreements.

An explicit distinction between GBS and non-GBS donors must be made here. Although this chapter focuses on GBS donors, both as a group and individually, the influence of non-GBS donors is of interest, as it has an impact on the engagement of GBS donors. The increasing international influence of China and the rise of other non-OCED-DAC donors (discussed in Chapter 4) has increased the availability of foreign aid and investment from non-OCED-DAC donors and non-GBS donors. Mirroring the increase of China's global influence, its relationship with Tanzania is strengthening. The mutual advantage brought by China's ability to provide Tanzania with the capital, skills and technology to access natural gas reserves in exchange for access to those resources, is openly discussed (Xiaoqing and Calkins 2013). This has affected the relationship between the Tanzanian government and GBS donors, reducing the latter's bargaining power. There has been a corresponding increase in interest in China's strategy among GBS donors.[7]

---

7    The interest of GBS donors in China has been seen in the interest generated in the work of a visiting Chinese academic to Dar es Salaam in June 2010 and the United Kingdom's interest in developing a partnership with China to deliver aid to Tanzania (Hawksley and Mikwambe 2010).

We argue that procedural accountability has increased to the meet the demands of the international aid agenda, but it also coexists with relational accountability. In Chapter 4 we found non- OECD-DAC donors employ an approach to accountability that sits more firmly in the relational realm. This can be seen in the absence of both formalised reporting mechanisms and broad conditionalities for disbursing aid. Instead, any conditions are related more closely to the specific contract under which they provide their aid, such as the donor's contractors being used to deliver services (tied aid).

Tanzania's foreign policy relations with its donors clearly reflect domestic interests. Internal and external demands for democratisation during Mwinyi's presidency saw increasing procedural accountability and started the process of opening-up to democracy. Mkapa legitimised CCM whilst maintaining the relational links between business and politics. There was a movement towards self-reliance instead of coercion, as liberal state building involved seeking increased legitimacy from donors, combined with increased procedural accountability, which in turn allowed donors to fulfil their interests to disburse increased amounts of aid. Kikwete's stronger domestic focus, at the expense of the GBS donors, reflected his roots and background; it was also motivated by the need to juggle domestic networks of support for political stability. Access to new sources of finance provided some independence from OECD-DAC donors and the GBS group.

After 2005, there was an increasing focus on relational accountability interests with the domestic realm. To what extent does this more explicit focus on the domestic coalition have an impact on the relationship with GBS donors?

*Dialogue and the Donor-government Relationship*

While some informal relationships between the government and donors have been maintained, there has been a general move towards a more formalised aid relationship, guided by the international aid agenda. Interviews with donors, direct personal observations and the documents supporting GBS point to the increasing formalisation of the donor-government relationship and deterioration in the nature of the relationship in terms of access to information and cordiality of relations.[8]

The changes in the nature of the dialogue between donors and government can be characterised by a pendulum, which swings between different levels of trust. Between 2000 and 2002 was the period of the establishment of GBS and of the development of harmonised GBS conditionality infrastructure. During this time, donors closely monitored the implementation of the budget and built the basis for the higher trust equilibrium that followed. Between 2002 and 2004 there was a honeymoon period of high and increasing trust on both sides. From 2004 to 2005, corresponding to the final year of Mkapa's presidency, saw a reduction of interest among donors in the technical activities of government. However,

---

8    Interviews took place mainly in 2009 and the author's work and personal observations on GBS and aid to Tanzania have been on-going since 2000.

policies continued to be negotiated and steered at the political level (in the Heads of Cooperation Forum). The international aid agenda was implemented from 2006 onwards, and this saw an increased focus on monitoring results and growth in the harmonisation infrastructure. The government became more inwardly focused as the Kikwete presidency established itself, a trend which has persisted. The relationship has experienced increasing instances of conflict, some of which were fuelled by corruption scandals.

Kikwete's more explicit emphasis on domestic networks has been evidenced by the removal of senior civil servants from positions where they were successfully interacting with donors, to positions where they were more (and often entirely) focused on issues outside the arena of foreign aid. The removal of key players, particularly from the Ministry of Finance, has increased the frustration of donors and arguably contributed to the increasing conflict around ratings of performance. Instances of conflict from 2007 onwards can be considered in terms of red lines, with donors challenged to continue to release GBS or becoming frustrated to the point of having to make a stand and requiring a positive response from the government. While the government has responded to these situations in a manner that has allowed for the continued disbursement of GBS, recent reductions in GBS allocations are a reflection of the increasing dissatisfaction donors are voicing alongside changes in aid policy in donor headquarters.[9]

The perspective taken on nature of the donor–government relationship is highly dependent on when the starting point is. For instance, if we take a longer-term perspective, from the time of the Helleiner Report in 1995, suggests that the relationship has been strong enough to withstand disputes around the abuse of power and the misuse of funds, with varying periods of high and low trust at the individual level. An important aspect of the individual relationship between donors and government is the way messages are communicated, which is central to the outcome achieved. It can be challenging to communicate in an effective way:

> So much comes down to ... personality. This cannot be faked. Pushiness doesn't necessarily result in the required results but if you are nice you possibly don't get the results either. However, if you're pushy then you may not get the results and then relations are harmed too. (Interview with government technical assistant, Ministry of Finance 2004–2007, July 2009)

However, any perspective on the dialogue is highly subjective: it is a function of expectations and rooted in the context of short-term episodes. As donors spend a great deal of time talking to each other – and increasingly so in the context of

---

9    The balance between the two is difficult to determine as feedback is bi-directional. The rise of the results agenda, supported by political changes in some donor countries, has certainly had an impact on GBS. However, as we see below conflict started to increase before the changes within some donor agencies.

implementing the harmonised aid architecture – they reinforce their own perspectives and strengthen the collective the thinking of the group, as we will now turn to.

## 6.4  Power and the Aid Relationship

The power relations between donors and government can be represented in their interactions around the disbursement of GBS and the review of progress in the performance framework. By drawing out occurrences that illustrate a procedural and relational understanding of power we can conceptualise procedural power as a limited resource that is contractual and rests with the principal or the agent. In contrast, relational power is ubiquitous and unlimited – a process that latently underpins all interactions. Its ideological representation through language and its subtle underpinning of communication is important for understanding how the dialogue that takes place between donors and government has the potential to shape views and policy. The question of recipient government leadership and ownership has continually been raised and debated in donor circles. The second-generation poverty reduction strategy papers (PRSPs) were developed to increase government ownership, yet they embody an externally developed neoliberal agenda: just as the first generation PRSPs were developed to obtain debt relief (Rweyemamu 2009), the second generation ones were necessary to ensure the continuation of aid. Two issues of primary concern determine the extent of recipient government ownership: 1) the balance of power capacity between donors and government; and 2) the role of different groups within the recipient government. To examine the enactment of power, we apply the conditionality analysis from Chapter 4, and the discussion of the relational concept of power from Chapter 3, to the Tanzanian context.

GBS has evolved to be based on three main contractual mechanisms: 1) a joint memorandum between donors and government (the Partnership Framework Memorandum); 2) the Performance Assessment Framework (PAF); and 3) individual agreements between donors and the government. The performance framework for budget-support conditionality, the PAF, is procedural in nature, as it detracts from the substantive and often political issues affecting development. In doing so, it restricts the involvement of donors in policy dialogue to technical issues, even in higher-level forums (interviews with donors in 2009). The level of detail embodied in the PAF, which has contained more than 80 actions, has generally resulted in higher transaction costs, intrusion that reduces national ownership and a 'technocratic focus which militates against political input' (Booth et al. 2004: 49).[10] The procedural nature of the instrument is accompanied by a relational style of implementation, as there has sometimes been collaboration between donors and government, and between the Ministry of Finance and sector ministries, to achieve satisfactory ratings, despite performance being poor. Further

---

10    Although the PAF was streamlined in 2012/13 these weaknesses persist.

negotiation and strategising takes place as working groups can update and propose new indicators for the following year.

## Power, Donors and Conditionality

Following the discussion of conditionality in Chapter 4 that described the different interests of donors and the recipient government, we model aid delivery as a bargaining game in Tanzania, capturing the influence of power relations and associated incentives.

Table 6.3 applies the six objectives of conditionality (Collier and Gunning 1996 cited in White and Morrissey 1997: 498) to aid programmes in Tanzania, identifying examples that fall into each of the objectives including the IMF's Poverty Reduction and Growth Facility (PRGF), the European Commission (EC) Millennium Contract for budget support and the World Bank's Poverty Reduction Support Credit (PRSC). A number of the objectives refer to the monitoring of performance using the PAF, such as monitoring and signalling through outcome indicators, and paternalism and bribery in relation to the variable tranches. Technical assistance is perhaps the clearest example of the supportive objective. However, in many cases it is difficult to distinguish between paternalism and bribery, and to do so requires a further consideration of the motivations behind the intentions to bribe the government to change its behaviour. Understanding the supportive aspect of aid requires a degree of abstraction from the other objectives, as almost all aid could be argued to be supportive. However, the question is the extent to which this dominates as an objective.

The outcome of conditionality is determined by bargaining, which depends on how well the recipient can play the game of agreeing to the tighter conditionality, whilst knowing slippage will result. This in turn raises the issue of the credibility of conditionality in a repeated game (discussed in Chapter 4). The recipient can use slippage as a strategy by agreeing to a tighter conditionality than it is actually willing to implement. This presents a credibility dilemma to donors – should they punish slippage in accordance with the conditionality agreement or to disburse anyway and increase utility? We can assess this by considering how the PAF has been used.

Coverage of the PAF broadened the content of policy discussions and became the tool through which donors monitored, and often attempted to influence, policy. The stated aim of the PAF – to 'prioritise existing targets and measures and link their achievement to the provision of budgetary support' (URT 2001: 3) – underestimates its usage, as the donor agenda has been pushed forward through some PAF actions. This leads the government to retain space in policy formulation and reform in three ways: 1) through maintaining a strategic ambiguity, whereby some room to manoeuvre is retained through ambiguity in reform commitments, which creates the space for later reneging on agreements and pursuing policies that may be in conflict with the assumptions underlying the commitments

**Table 6.3     The objectives of conditionality in aid programmes in Tanzania**

| Objectives of conditionality | Examples of the objectives found in Tanzania | | |
|---|---|---|---|
| | IMF PRGF | EC variable tranche – Millennium Contract | World Bank PRSC |
| 1. Paternalism | Letter of Intent | Joint donor–government working group to set indicators and targets; donors dominant owing to capacity constraints in government | |
| 2. Bribery | Letter of Intent – a focus on certain reforms/areas | Variable tranche to improve and focus on performance in certain areas | Prior action – a focus on certain reforms/areas |
| 3. Restraint | Inflation | | |
| 4. Signalling | Gatekeeper for GBS donors | Outcome indicators in the PAF | |
| 5. Monitoring | IMF PRGF missions | *Ex-post* monitoring of performance against indicators | Prior action review missions have taken place separately |
| 6. Supportive | Technical assistance via the East Africa Regional Technical Assistance Centre | Technical assistance provided in policy areas where there are common interests | |

*Note:* 1) paternalism – donors believing they know what is best for the recipient; 2) bribery – persuading the recipient to change behaviour; 3) restraint – recipient agrees to reforms and conditionalities prevent policy reversal; 4) signalling – that the reform programme is genuine; 5) monitoring – to ensure aid is having the intended effects; and 6) supportive – provided needed financing for reforms.
*Source:* Adapted from Collier and Gunning's (1996) framework.

(Richey 1999); 2) through slippage in implementation; and 3) through policy reversal. It is through these routes that the influence of donors is restrained.[11]

---

11    It should be noted that these are *ex-post* responses, and take place in the context of limited capacity in government. Where government capacity is greater, a preferred response would be *ex-ante*, staying a step ahead of donors and being able to make either policy proposals or clear responses to donor proposals.

## Power and Aid in the Tanzanian Government

In the context of a strategic game, the use of GBS is one of the few tools donors have to send signals to the government. Reduced acceptance of the neoliberal consensus forged by President Mkapa was apparent in calls for reduced dependence on donors and the ability to pursue policies of Tanzania's own choosing. This was vocalised by politicians from all parties as well as academics. For the Tanzanian government, slow progress in reform implementation disguised other interests and allegiances, and, while this domestic focus could be argued to be a display of government leadership, the real motivating factor is the need to maintain accountability to internal party factions and ensure protection of the interests of influential members of the elite.

Highlighting the role of different groups within the Tanzanian government helps to clarify not just the operation of different interests but also the conflicts of interests, and to stress that the government should not be viewed as a homogeneous entity. Costello (1996) notes the differing extent of influence of donors in the case of the Ministry of Agriculture and Livestock and the National Development Corporation. They found that in the Ministry of Agriculture and Livestock foreign aid was accompanied by 'carrots and sticks' to influence policy (Costello 1996: 137). This was less so in the case of the National Development Corporation, which pointed to a variance of views across different government agencies in the context of their retention of autonomy, given the failure of the state to define its role.

An example of this can be found in the public expenditure review sector evaluations. These were supported by the Ministry of Finance but resisted by some sectors, which saw them as creating more work but not feeding into budget negotiations, despite that being their aim. Insufficient capacity to coordinate policy implementation results in chaos within government: the common objectives captured in the documents that outline the plans and strategies for development sit in sharp contrast with the lack of coordination among the agents required to implement the policies (Hyden and Mmuya 2008). This highlights the differing views held within government and the lack of representativeness of the donor-friendly group of senior officials within the Ministry of Finance. Such 'donor-friendlies' are situated in the elite group and help maintain the illusion of consensus and mutual dependency with donors.

Such examples illustrate that leadership is not broad and unified but tussles take place between different groups in government. The leadership associated with GBS consists of a small cooperative elite centred in the Ministry of Finance. Eyben (2007: 28) referred to this as 'group think' and Fleck (1979) and Douglas (1986) as a 'thought collective' (Douglas 1986: 12): a specific thought style whereby a mutually reinforcing perspective and dialogue are embedded among a small group of donors and a small group of government officials. It is from within this elite group of officials that aid policies and development management discourse that will appeal to donors is predicted (Harrison and Mulley 2007). Bigsten (2001) has gone further to suggest policymakers anticipate which policies would appeal to donors and create their own policies on this premise. Harrison and Mulley (2007) identify two characteristics of the absence of a broad leadership base: a rise in the small group of officials who directly benefit from aid (via the perks of workshops and international travel) and with whom the donors feel most comfortable working; and the cultural effect of aid on Tanzanian governance, which is largely self-reinforcing and exists to ensure its own reproduction. These were specific characteristics of Mkapa's neoliberal agenda. 'The government knows how to play donors' (interview with economic advisor, multilateral donor agency, July 2009).

What the interface between clientelism (an aspect of relational accountability) and the formal, rule-based environment of the good governance agenda in which aid is delivered and the national budget is prepared (aspects of procedural accountability)? There is anecdotal evidence of the continuing intervention of senior officials, ministers and presidents in day-to-day affairs, such that formal rules are frequently pushed aside. In the context of weak administration and inadequate capacity that prevents the following of rules, such an approach can be more effective for policy implementation.

What implications do the good governance agenda and Tanzania's changing aid modalities have for the maintenance of political alliances and the payments local politicians can make to their constituents to secure their support? How do rewards evolve in response to changes in public financial management processes that are related to aid? An example of the changes taking place is the benefits in kind being offered for good performance, such as clean audits being rewarded by feasts (Kelsall 2008). Other examples can be found in the growth of allowances and workshops, with the associated benefits of *per diems*, meals and transport funding. In 2009/10 such allowances were estimated to be equivalent of one third of the wage bill and 11 per cent of the government's total recurrent expenditure.[12]

The civil service reform component of the good governance agenda has focused on increasing salaries for public servants and the removal of *per diems*. However, this has been pursued without consideration of the wider social context and the blurred interface of the public and the private. The extended family, at the core of African society, is often the recipient of increased salaries of public servants, and it is only through benefits such as meals, transport and *per diems* that the civil servants themselves can retain the benefits and therefore may be motivated to improve their performance (Kelsall 2008). This is yet another example of the imposition of a procedural approach to reforms that is in conflict with the more pervasive relational context, where the extended family or circle of trust dominates and personal networks are central to the functioning of the state.

The government has effectively had *carte blanche* since 2000. The conditions accompanying aid have been accepted yet, if they have not been in line with the government's own development agenda, they have not been fully met. As the international aid agenda has pushed forward the formal, and as the government has become more domestically focused, the quality of interactions between donors

---

12    Allowances were estimated to be Tsh 571 billion in 2009/10 (Policy Forum 2009b).

and government has declined. How has this been reflected in the PAF, the main instrument of conditionality for GBS donors?

*Power and Conflict in the PAF*

As the PAF has become the central focus for negotiations around GBS, it is a common source of instances of disagreement or even conflict. Alongside non-GBS support to accountability initiatives that we summarised above, accountability itself has been represented in the PAF as it has taken a more prominent place in the policies of interest to donors. Interestingly, as we saw earlier, this presents an internal contradiction with policies such as the removal of the development levy and support for large infrastructure companies, which have the potential to facilitate clientelism, alongside the increased availability of finance for rent seeking provided through GBS (Tripp, 2012).

There has been a change in the understanding of, and focus on, accountability in the PAF, together with a recognition that state institutions such as parliament own accountability, and an increased domestic accountability focus through the big reform programmes. This has increasingly integrated dialogue between government and donors into existing national processes. Progress on meeting accountability conditionalities was less than the average performance on PAF implementation for Tanzania and was influenced by the methodological challenge of measuring governance performance and the susceptibility of the sector to variances in corruption perceptions. This is indicative of the 'internationally acknowledged dilemma on how to measure governance in general' and the fact that accountability episodes or events such as corruption cases 'impact greatly on accountability perception[s], but can hardly be quantified' (Development Partner Governance Working Group 2008: 21).

Instances of disagreement between donors and government can be identified, but when does this move beyond negotiation to the point of becoming conflict? Negotiation arises during a dialogue that aims to agree on the amount of progress that has been achieved, assessed against pre-determined outcomes. For some donors this determines the proportion of their performance tranche that will be disbursed. While this negotiation process might involve episodes of disagreement, when overall agreement cannot be reached it escalates into conflict which is characterised by incompatibility and a belief that the interests of those involved are opposed.

Disagreement around GBS and the PAF can be thought of in terms of cognitive dissonance between the two groups. Donors may create tension in order to raise an issue of non-performance in discussions with government. There can also be dissonance within government between the demands of the domestic constituency and policies that are being implemented. Four different types of disagreement or conflict have occurred.

*Type 1: Where expectations of policy implementation in the PAF have not been met*
The challenging crop board prior action that required the approval of a strategy
for the reform of at least two crop boards is such an example. This involved a shift
from the government managing the crop boards to 'supporting private sector led
growth to enhance the competitiveness of Tanzania's main agricultural exports'
(World Bank 2005: 24). This resulted in both a reduction of $25 million in the
World Bank's PRSC3 disbursement in 2005 (World Bank 2005) and the later
rewording and rolling over of the action in the PAF until 2008, when it was passed
by parliament (World Bank 2005, World Bank 2008).

*Type 2: Where PAF policies have been implemented despite domestic objection*
Donor proposals for the method and timing of the privatisation of the National
Bank of Commerce and the National Microfinance Bank were rejected by the
Finance and Economic Affairs Committee of parliament, yet the proposals were
still implemented due to excessive donor influence (Mmari et al 2005).

*Type 3: Where GBS has been delayed or changed owing to an issue outside the PAF*
The external payment account corruption case illustrates conflict between donors
and the executive resulting from weaknesses in public financial management
systems and processes. In 2008/09, budget-support disbursements equivalent
to 12 per cent of the budget were delayed by three months, as donors requested
responses to questions concerning the follow-up to auditors' recommendations
(ThisDay 2008a, 2008b, URT 2008a). Following this conflict, the government
felt it had taken sufficient steps to show willingness and to appease the donors,
although donors withheld GBS disbursements for 2007/08 until the last minute
as an expression of their dissatisfaction. By threatening to not release funds, the
donors were in direct contravention of their agreement with the government,
stepping outside their own increasingly formalised framework. This led to concern
over the stability of the budget and a subsequent reduction in trust between
government and donors.

*Type 4: Disagreement in the PAF rating between donors and government*
Instances of disagreement occurred once in 2007; twice in 2008; and six times
in 2007, the overall rating for 'Cluster Working Group (CWG) 3: Governance
and Accountability' was disputed, with government considering progress to be
satisfactory and donors that it was 'fair moving' (URT2007a: 101). In 2008,
donors and government could not agree on an overall rating for 'CWG 1: Growth
and Poverty Reduction', with the government applying a satisfactory rating and
donors labelling it unsatisfactory. In 2009, there was disagreement not only over the
more subjective underlying processes but also around a temporary process action
and an outcome indicator. Once again, there was discord over the ratings of the
underlying processes – for Business Environment Strengthening for Tanzania, and
additionally the energy sector review, the Local Government Reform Programme
and the Public Financial Management Reform Programme.

This analysis illustrates how the apparent procedural accountability rating system for the PAF embodies key relational accountability characteristics. Although the rating system gives the impression of being objective, it is often not possible to state clearly whether an action has been achieved or not. The result of this element of subjectivity is that the different personalities involved in making the assessments in the working groups play a role, and typically the views of those with more power and a more senior position in the hierarchy are deferred to.

This examination of the different types of conflict around GBS demonstrates the different strategies that may be employed to recoup some policy space. The PAF emerged so donors could be actively involved in the prioritisation of policy measures, using the 'carrot' of financing as an incentive; however, our discussion of the use of the PAF demonstrates that the government effectively negotiates policy space. Several interviewees spoke of the government's negotiation strategy:

> The government pays lip service to donor policy and carries out its own policy anyway (interview with governance advisor, bilateral donor agency, July 2009).

> Donors attached values [to indicators] and cut funding; therefore the government tried to get less included in PAF (interview with government technical assistant, Ministry of Finance 2004–2007, July 2009).

> The government colludes with the sector ministries to get good reviews for the PAF. There's no substance to discussions as it's mainly disputes about ratings (interview with economic advisor, bilateral donor agency, July 2009).

While the PAF is rooted firmly in procedural accountability, and this is increasingly the dominant approach of donors, an element of relational accountability does exist, as negotiations and collaboration take place between donors and government. In many cases, despite conflict being present, the incentives for donors to disburse dominate.

The first type of conflict is where expectations of policy implementation in the PAF are not met and policy space is recouped through slippage. This can either result in disbursement as donors acquiesce; alternatively, a small proportion of GBS funding may be forgone. Scope for subjectivity exists in the wording of actions, difficulties encountered that may be outside the control of the government, and changes in the implementation process.

Although conflict may exist, collusion also sometimes takes place to obtain a satisfactory rating of the GBS review. This was particularly prevalent prior to 2005. The existence of collaboration between donors and government implies a game is being played, and this requires that a positive relationship exists; either that, or it may be inferred and simply exist owing to a coincidence of interests.

## 6.5  Summary: Aid as a Reflection of Sociopolitical Relations

This chapter has analysed the provision of aid, specifically GBS, in Tanzania and has placed it in a broader perspective where it is part of the pattern of relations shaped by social context and historical episodes. It has built on the state and society analysis undertaken in Chapter 5 to present an examination of the changing pattern of aid dependency, conditionality and negotiation and power relations between donors and government in Tanzania. The discussion has pointed towards the coexistence of the procedural and relational aspects of accountability, and has highlighted cases where the increasingly formal procedural elements are not aligned with the more pervasive higher-level relational structures.

The recent history of foreign policy and donor-government relations presents a picture of underlying tensions, although these have frequently been prevented from having an impact on external relations. Firstly under Nyerere, but also under later presidents, a careful path has been trod around issues with the potential to present challenges to the foreign aid relationship. It is at times that challenges have arisen that the stance of governments and donors – and the style of their interactions – have been most interesting.

As aid inflows to Tanzania increased under the reformist presidency of Mkapa, there were increasing demands in terms of the resources required to manage and report on funds and to maintain a dialogue with donors. This saw the emergence of a core group of senior officials, concentrated in the Ministry of Finance and the President's Office. Such officials played the role of trusted individuals, to which much of the donor confidence in Tanzania can be attributed. Behind this external façade, tussles between different groups in government persisted. During Kikwete's first term, he focused on international policy and retreated from the sphere of GBS donors to instead respond to domestic coalitions. This was one of the factors that led to the deterioration of the government's relationship with GBS donors. The increasing availability of finance from other donors, free of dialogue and conditionalities, as well as expectations of future hydrocarbon revenues, has increasingly filled the space previously occupied by GBS donors. This has reduced the bargaining power of GBS donors.

These changes in Tanzania's foreign policy relations with donors have in common the consistent reflection of domestic interests. International demands to democratise during Mwinyi's presidency coincided with the start of multiparty democracy. Mkapa's era of international re-politicisation further legitimised CCM and co-opted the business elite into the core of the state elite. The recent move towards policies with a more explicit domestic focus, as pursued by Kikwete, has been influenced by the need to respond to domestic clients who are less reformist and more socialist in their outlook than those to whom Mkapa was responding. Here we see the pursuit of both explicit vote winning strategies through the provision of visible public goods and policies such as Kilimo Kwanza (Agriculture First), alongside clientelistic payoffs to maintain local level capture.

The annual assessment of the PAF provides the negotiating forum between government and donors and is therefore the arena in which power is demonstrated and exercised. It is here that challenges in the implementation of big reform programmes are highlighted. While the PAF has increased the procedural focus on accountability initiatives, the provision of increased finance for rent seeking through GBS, the removal of the development levy and support for large infrastructure companies, all contradict this as these measures have the potential to facilitate clientelism (Tripp, 2012).

The PAF itself is procedural in nature, although it is accompanied by a relational style of implementation, which disguises other interests and allegiances, maintaining accountability to internal party factions and ensuring the interests of influential actors are protected. Tanzania has pursued a strategy of slippage and strategic ambiguity, presenting a credibility dilemma for donors. It is through this that *de jure* policy has differed from *de facto* implementation.

# Chapter 7
# A New Approach to Foreign Aid for Tanzania

## 7.1 Introduction

This book has deconstructed what we mean by accountability through an analysis of its epistemological assumptions. We have critiqued the traditional understanding of accountability; that is, procedural accountability, which focuses on formal contractual mechanisms that are rooted in a principal-agent approach. This approach sees problems as one-sided, and misses a fuller understanding of how accountability operates in complex social contexts, where all parties are facing constraints and the problem is rather how actors can 'act collectively in their own best interests' to find solutions (Booth 2012: 11). Relational accountability is embedded within the personal relations between actors who, in turn, respond to social norms. It takes a longer-term perspective and is characterised by rules that can be informal and highly complex and accidental, and that may have evolved over a period of time.

Our new understanding is built on insights from economics, sociology, anthropology, psychology, political theory and philosophy that allow us to move beyond the limiting assumptions that constrain the traditional understanding of accountability. In deconstructing the assumptions underlying concepts of accountability, we move towards an understanding where both procedural and relational accountability operate together. As relational accountability is a deeper and more durable concept, it frames the operation of the more transient procedural accountability. When the demands of donors, which are in the form of procedural accountability, are discordant with the nature of relational accountability, conflict ensues. There are restrictions that the higher-level relational accountability imposes on the lower procedural level too; namely, where the particular cultural setting restricts the range of governance institutions that can be accepted within a particular society and, in turn, dictates those that function successfully. Discord results where a change is imposed that does not accord with the higher-level structures.

This theory is illustrated by a case study of Tanzania, one the largest recipients of aid in sub-Saharan Africa. Focusing on the public sector at the national level, we have considered the rise and fall of general budget support. In the international aid environment, there is a meeting of actors from different cultures, operating within a non-Western societal context. With due caution – we cannot generalise from one case study – we find that the fall of general budget support in Tanzania does emphasise the necessity of restructuring aid delivery around an understanding of relational accountability that is specific to each country; in order to deepen our appreciation of accountability beyond the procedural.

## 7.2   Relational and Procedural Accountability

If an occurrence arises through procedural accountability that does not fit within the boundaries of the higher-level relational accountability, discord will result. This can lead to conflict in the form of game playing and the rejection of the procedural accountability demand or a shift in the relational accountability framework, seen in the analyses of general budget support (GBS) conditionalities in Chapter 6.

Both the interaction between, and mutual dependency of, the two types of accountability are key to understanding relations between donors and government. Procedural accountability is imposed as a tool, and one through which donors understand the development context. It is also embodied in processes; however, its operation is always tempered by the relational accountability context. This is made manifestly clear by considering how the two may operate in isolation. If the procedural understanding is applied in isolation there is no analysis of the highly context specific and complex cultural factors that underlie the relationships around which accountability is formed. This results in the impossibility of understanding the motivations and the incentives of actors and, in turn, understanding their responses to different scenarios (a typical frustration amongst donors). However, if only the relational accountability framework is applied, the ability to comprehend both shorter-term progress and more direct accountability, and to frame our immediate context, is diminished (a limitation that can be found amongst recipient civil servants). By extension, the two types of accountability must be complementary and must co-exist.

However, they can also be in conflict if the demands of procedural accountability extend beyond the current framework of relational accountability. This results in either the resolution of the conflict at the procedural level, so that the demands of one party are refuted, or it may result in the procedural demands being accommodated by an evolution in the relational accountability characteristics. Such an adjustment in the higher-level relational characteristics is unusual, as these are the highly embedded attributes, such as social norms, customs and other complex informal institutions, which – as Williamson (2000) outlined – can take millennia to change.

This work has presented a perspective on power and the elite that underpins the conceptualisation of relational accountability; it helps to describe how networks are structured, how influence is exerted, and how co-optation takes place. Elites are pivotal in formulating policies and taking decisions, and in linking the state and society, because they reach out in a web-like structure. They capture the interests of actors as they function within a multitude of different social roles within different networks. As elite factions compete for, and co-opt, actors from society, they mirror institutional structures in wider society, and personal and social patterns of interaction. The political leadership is intertwined within these structures of power and legitimacy. The operation of clientelistic relations, based on informal rules, depends upon retaining the network of support of elites; that is, embedding actors, and providing the knowledge and the respect that facilitates the fulfilment of their designated roles (Evans et al. 1996, Kelsall et al. 2010). Such networks are crucial to the functioning of the state.

This web-like structure reflects the often apparent contradictions in people's behaviour; the variability in responses and roles in reaction to the complex reality on the ground does not easily fit into the procedural notion of accountability. Specifically, the notion of elites and their role in society does not fit well with the traditional procedural notion of accountability, which provides no space for the differential influence, through power, of different groups. Our use of the term 'structure' is not to imply that it is constant or fixed; rather that, as different agents and different groups exert different influences at different times, elites are fluid, mirroring the dynamism of social relations. This allows a movement away from the assumption embodied within procedural accountability that there is equality across actors and that society is simply an aggregation of individual preferences, and therefore highly impersonal in nature.

## 7.3   Case-study Findings

*The Sociopolitical Context in Tanzania*

Our case study of Tanzania has examined how the clientelist politics of the domestic sphere, dominated by relational accountability characteristics, cohabits with the increasingly formal international arena, which uses procedural accountability as its dominant framework. While there have been increasing efforts of donors to understand the complexities of country politics in recent years, the neoliberal agenda has, in the past, excluded the complex social context of the domestic sphere. The focus upon the formal, the contractual, the measurable and the rational is frequently incompatible with the wider sociopolitical and economic context. Aid most effectively supports reform where there is a coincidence between donor and recipient interests such that the conditions do not invoke a conflict between the formal conditions in the procedural realm and the higher-level relational context.

The increasingly formalised international aid environment of the Paris Declaration and the Accra Agenda for Action is juxtaposed with the relational context that frames the dances between donors and government. At times, it appears as though there are two governments in operation: the government with its external face for donors; and the government with its internal face and concerns, where the party dominates. It is by looking at this internal face that the importance of distribution can be seen, whereby the government spreads out resources to maintain the support of its clients. This is an aspect of relational accountability that represents accountability to powerful actors (including elites), and which is necessary for the survival of the state. It remains the case that the private extended family is the primary circle of concern where payoffs are made; however, the same concept can be applied to the maintenance of political and business alliances (which can be considered to be the public extended family).

Chama Cha Mapinduzi's (CCM) dominance as the ruling party has continued (Khan and Gray 2006), despite the increasing influence of the opposition. This is due to CCM's success in limiting the mobilisation of society, through both the marginalisation of civil society and the operation of networks of relational accountability. This influence is supported by media support for CCM; election financing; the use of public resources for campaigning; the state security apparatus, which favours CCM; legislative restrictions on forming coalitions; the banning of independent candidacy; and special seat allocations.

Recently, political stability and patterns of rent seeking have begun to change as increasing fragmentation within the ruling party has become apparent in the rising voices of CCM factions. The increasing prominence of the opposition political parties on the mainland has supported these CCM factions; they are provided with a credible route for defection, increasing their ability to both demand and seek rents (Kelsall 2013). These separatist tendencies have been supported by an incentive to tolerate rent seeking and the growth of CCM capitalism, at the same time as CCM has successfully co-opted and facilitated businesses, which, in turn, provide rents for the party. This has become increasingly important in an environment of both increasing political competition and increasing costs of participating in elections (Cooksey 2011, Kelsall and Mmuya 2005). This rent-seeking activity involves a reduction in the provision of public goods and also the efficiency of public expenditure. This occurs in three ways, as discussed in Chapter 5: firstly, through CCM's country-wide vote-mobilisation strategy, which involves focusing on the provision of only highly visible public goods which may divert provision from less visible goods that are, however, no less important; secondly, by returning favours from private sector actors by providing benefits through the evasion of taxation, which represents lost revenue, through contract acquisition, or through an adjustment in the allocation of public goods; and thirdly, through local level capture by politicians or local leaders providing goods to villages or wards in an attempt to secure their position. This sits within the realm of relational accountability, rather than that of formal and contractual procedural accountability. These patterns of clientelism have direct implications for civil society. Civil society has been both co-opted and restrained in Tanzania, owing to the plurality of different identities and the state's efforts to undermine attempts at collective organisation. Many of the non-governmental organisations that are engaged in dialogue with the executive have been co-opted and are themselves members of elites.

Public financial management reforms undertaken since the late 1990s have centralised the control of rents (Kelsall et al. 2013). The implementation of the programme has also experienced a number of challenges and delays, as could be expected for extensive reforms that directly challenge the organisation and control of rents. As would also be expected, areas of inefficiency persist. *De jure* policy differs from *de facto* implementation and effective 'policy' is actually determined during the implementation process (Lipsky 2010, Kjær and Therkildsen 2013).

## The Foreign Aid Context in Tanzania

This book has examined the dynamics of the relationship between general budget support (GBS) donors and government. It has analysed how power is demonstrated and exercised in the annual assessment of performance, in a matrix comprising policy actions and results (the Performance Assessment Framework). This monitoring system is the basis of the accountability relationship between donors and the Tanzanian government. The government has employed a strategy of slippage and strategic ambiguity to avoid conditionalities. This has been increasingly so in an environment of new sources of finance, which presents a credibility dilemma for donors. It is through this that *de jure* policy differs from *de facto* implementation. The framework itself is procedural in nature, although it is accompanied by a relational style of implementation, which disguises other interests and allegiances, maintaining accountability to internal party factions, and ensuring the protection of the interests of influential actors.

The history of foreign policy and relationships with donors presents a picture of underlying tensions. Under the presidency of Mkapa, these tensions were managed by a core group of senior officials, concentrated in the Ministry of Finance and Economic Affairs and the President's Office, to whom much of the donor confidence in Tanzania can be attributed. Behind this external façade, tussles between different groups in government persisted. President Kikwete's more focused international policy, and the retreat from the sphere of budget support donors as a response to domestic coalitions, has seen the pursuit of both explicit vote winning strategies through the provision of visible public goods and policies, such as Kilimo Kwanza, and clientelistic payoffs to maintain local level capture. The space to do this has been created by the increasing availability of finance from other donors (without dialogue and conditionalities attached), and expectations of future hydrocarbon revenues.

The stated aim of GBS donors has been to pursue policy objectives in line with both poverty reduction and the international aid agenda. The policy constraints of the latter have greatly influenced the behaviour of donors during the last decade. Broadly, drives to increase harmonisation and reduce transaction costs have resulted in an increased formalisation in the nature of dialogue with recipients, and an increased focus on results. Specifically, however, there has been the adoption of a common monitoring framework and a good governance agenda – two characteristics that reduce the degrees of freedom of GBS donors. Whilst relational characteristics are employed, these constraints have prevented these donors moving too far outside the procedural accountability framework.

Neither types of accountability exist in their pure forms. Both donors and the Tanzanian government employ behaviours that fit with both relational and procedural accountability when necessary, although they ultimately exhibit more signs of their dominant type. This dominance of procedural accountability amongst donors results in them looking above the surface and avoiding the reality of how state and society functions in Tanzania.[1] This is inappropriate to the Tanzanian context, where the need to maintain the support of the winning coalition in the context of a limited access order economy requires that redistribution takes place along patron-client networks (Khan 2004b, North et al. 2007, Lindemann and Putzel 2008). This results in the government being accountable to interests other than donors and in government accountability operating within a relationally dominant framework. As the framework that donors use is procedurally dominant, this results in them overlooking the importance of networks for the government, which are essential for ensuring that it maintains the political support necessary for a stable sociopolitical environment. Whilst stability is an important foreign policy objective of donors, the importance of relational accountability in achieving this is purposefully overlooked in the preference for procedural dominance in the implementation of aid.

This interaction between procedural and relational accountability is important and it is only through the consideration of how both function together that an understanding and a complete picture of how accountability works in Tanzania can be generated. Relational accountability is frequently either not considered at all or is perceived as representing negative influences that should be eliminated. Rarely is its centrality to the effective functioning of the Tanzanian state recognised by the donor community. Overlooking the relational aspect of accountability is detrimental to the understanding of how state and society works. This is not to present relational accountability as a catch-all that can explain all behaviours; rather, it is a new lens through which to look at the aid relationship, a lens that is more firmly rooted in the wider cultural and historical context. This understanding forms the basis of a new approach to aid.

### 7.4 Summary: Reflections on a New Approach to Foreign Aid

What does this tell us about the approach to aid? Building on the discussion of a new policy from Chapter 4, what specific attributes can be applied to Tanzania? The two core foreign policy objectives of security and domestic investment are unreconciled with the rhetoric of aid for most OECD-DAC donors. This dichotomy underpins the conflict in aid relationships that often results. The mainstream governance discourse looks at the importance of politics and the role for informal

---

1    A distinction should be made between what donors will formally express whilst representing their organisations and the understanding of some individuals, which goes much further and understands the limits to the procedurally dominant approach. This critique of the approach of donors is based on the formal expressions of the majority and therefore may not capture the more in-depth understanding of some.

institutions, yet, despite this, characteristics such as rent seeking and clientelism are still seen as 'pathologies' (Unsworth 2010: 6).

The policy implications emerging from this analysis do not correspond to donors' current mode of operation, and directly conflict with OECD-DAC donors' foreign policy, the need to report to domestic constituents and institutional constraints such as pressures to disburse. While we should not necessarily see the challenge of donors reporting to their domestic constituents as a binding constraint (see Glennie et al. 2012, with reference to the UK), the incentive structure in donor agencies is such that employees have to respond to their headquarters. This results in the pursuit of internal policy, and a style of delivery that is procedural in nature. This can also result in little account being taken of the recipient domestic context. Given the embeddedness of these constraints, they are only likely to be alleviated in the medium- or long-term, and only if a substantial internal shift takes place in donor agencies.

Other donors do not face such constraints, and the East Asian model (which includes the aid programmes of China, Japan and South Korea) offers a balance to the dominance of Northern and Western approaches (Urban et al. 2011b). For example, China's input is financial, often providing the resources to build infrastructure directly. Through this, it more efficiently overcomes any capacity gaps that would present challenges to the delivery of the investment and that might also damage China's commercial interest in accessing natural resources (de Haan and Warmerdam 2012). These donors operate more firmly in the relational accountability realm, as they neither require formalised reporting mechanisms nor broad conditionalities for disbursing aid. They are, however, more likely to require that aid is tied.

Bringing these incentives and constraints to the fore of discussions, and unbuttoning the cloak of rhetoric that surrounds aid, serve to increase our awareness of the various limitations of donor agencies. This implies a change in both the approach taken by donors and in the areas donors focus on, with implications for aid modalities. This call echoes those made by others (including Booth 2012, Andrews et al. 2012, Andrews 2013) to allow space for local actors to find solutions to development problems. This is similarly supported by literature that focuses on the relational approach and argues for a movement away from an understanding of aid and development that is rooted in Western experience (Gulrajani 2010, Unsworth 2010). There has been an intent to adjust amongst donors during the last decade, however, in many cases this has involved 'careful studies of each country context, followed by suggested remedies that remain well within the terms of the good governance philosophy, albeit with a different vocabulary, point of entry or timescale' (Booth 2012: 92).

Central to adopting a relational understanding is the concept of elites, specifically the ruling coalition; their influence upon development, and the constraints that they may present. Whilst there are characteristics of elites that cannot be influenced by donors and foreign aid, it is important to understand those areas where elite interests can positively impact upon development, and how to support such outcomes. Defining what is meant by positive outcomes through an application of the relational perspective to aid policy – and how such outcomes could be influenced by external actors – overlaps with the work of research programmes such as the Africa Power and Politics Programme and the Centre for the Future State.[2] This involves identifying the nature of the interface between state and business elites, and the implications that this may have for development outcomes. The fundamental role of individual, rather than institutional, drivers of development that exist in many countries should be acknowledged. In doing so, an understanding of who is likely to champion particular initiatives, as well as an understanding of their interests and connections should be developed. Such individuals who create pressures for change are, however, embedded within a number of different networks. It is the nature of these interrelationships and the tensions between actors in parliament, the business sector, the executive and wider society that shape incentives and, in turn, preferences for policy implementation.

---

2    Africa Power and Politics Programme (http://www.institutions-africa.org) and the Centre for the Future State (http://www2.ids.ac.uk/futurestate).

# Appendix 1

# The Epistemology of Relational Accountability

Drawing on anthropological and sociological approaches we reflect on the complexity of the environment. Rather than attempting to simplify findings into one objective truth – the approach dictated by orthodox economics – we allow for potentially numerous 'truths', with an awareness of emerging dominant themes. Our approach, borrowing from Alvesson et al. (2004: 3) is that 'data and facts are constructions that result from interpretation'. All data, and, subsequently, knowledge, are interpreted and are not neutral or apolitical, but are a function of context-specific language and ideology.

Taking a reflexive approach, our position was a primary consideration during the research, and attempts were made to consider explicitly how this position influenced the responses gained and the interpretations made. Reflexivity is based on the principle that knowledge is shaped through the social processes of the research field, which, in turn, are based on power, context and history. Alvesson (2004) notes that the choice of research topic, the framing of questions, and the methods chosen are influenced by fashion and reflect the orientations of a particular research community. The reflexive approach considers that any clear divisions between the research framework, the researcher and the data have been falsely constructed. Fine et al. (2000) identify the responsibilities of the researcher as understanding 1) our identities and the impact these may have on the research and subsequent findings; 2) why we interrogate what we do; 3) what we choose not to report; 4) how we frame data; and 5) who we focus on and why.

There are a number of different types of reflexive approach and accompanying methodologies. Alvesson et al. (2004) identify four: destabilising practices; multi-perspective practices; multi-voicing practices; and positioning practices. We focus on the multi-voicing and positioning practices here. The former recognises that the researcher is neither neutral nor objective, and recognises the location of knowledge. Methods and writings aim to reduce the authority of the researcher and author and to allow other voices to permeate, in doing so recognising the relationship between the researcher and the research subject and allowing the reader a more active role in interpretation (Alvesson et al. 2004). The methods employed include also focusing on the researcher as a subject and recognising that the self of the researcher is *created* in the field (Reinharz 1997), leading to reporting on the experiences of the researcher as personal disclosure, which, for example, explains the avoidance of certain premises or points of view.

The reflexive approach has a number of difficulties. First, it is subject to interpretation, and readers' interpretations are a function of what the researcher chooses to present. Second, it contains a number of paradoxes: for example, it is based on there being no determinate conclusion, yet it still aims to point towards one; and the researcher is portrayed as a superior navigator of 'the social forces which shape the knowledge production process', yet such forces are considered un-navigable (Alvesson et al. 2004: 12). Third, it is possible to get caught in a 'loop of relativism' (Alvesson et al. 2004: 7), in which the more we think we know, the less reflexive we are; yet, as all knowledge is provisional (and constructed), the more reflexive we are, the less we can know.

Applying an effective reflexive approach in the research necessary for this book involved understanding the factors influencing the research, and being explicit about positioning, ranging from academic and professional positioning, to the cultural and physical. This was necessary to understand first how the researcher may have been perceived by, and in turn may have influenced, the research subjects, and how this may have biased the findings; and second, how bias may have been introduced through the researcher's interpretations of both the environment and the secondary and primary data.

Having worked for the Tanzanian government and for international aid organisations in Dar es Salaam both as staff (an insider) and as a consultant (an outsider), my professional background offered the possibility of 'liminality', an anthropological term referring to the ability to hover on the threshold (Eyben 2009: 2): to be 'positioned as neither insider nor outsider, retaining the empathy for the insider's position while sufficiently distant to cultivate a critical faculty'. It should also be noted that this professional background predisposed me to make interpretations in line with the dominant culture of the aid industry. It also presented a greater challenge in relation to being sensitive to elements that, given my earlier, long-term immersion in the Tanzanian context, I might overlook through normalisation. A failure to identify certain characteristics of the environment, because of an inability to distance oneself from the research surroundings, can result in researcher bias. To minimise this risk, I attempted to be vigilant against any tendencies not to question interview responses and emerging explanations resulting from a perceived understanding of the environment.

The hierarchy of importance of these personal, academic and professional characteristics is a function of the specific research environment. This leads to considerations of the ability we have to present ourselves in certain ways to influence the researcher–subject relationship, which can be manipulated but not eliminated. It may be that we wish to introduce a more equal relationship between the researcher and the subject; depending on the relative status of each, this may involve subtly either elevating or reducing our own status, and attempting to appear as similar to the subject as possible to put them at ease. Related to this are ethical considerations: small changes may naturally take place as we attempt to put respondents at ease; however, large changes that involve lying or invoking a disguise are, of course, to be resisted, as they are dishonest.

In the Tanzanian context, reflexivity was used to prevent the reproduction of buzzwords or dominant vocabulary without reflection, in a research area whose status is supported by, and meanings are mystified through, the extensive use of jargon and acronyms (examples given by Cornwall 2007 include 'good governance', 'anti-corruption', 'poverty' and 'civil society'). It was also applied to deconstruct the influences that the researcher's background would necessarily have had on the research, and to produce more honest findings that could contribute to an increased understanding of the aid context, which could not have been gained through a more positivist approach.

In summary, a reflexive methodological approach to studying accountability and budget support recognises the location of knowledge, how the self is created in the field (multi-voicing) and how social processes shape knowledge and the position of influence of the researcher. Using this approach enabled continued awareness of assumptions being made and the maintenance of liminality, or the ability to 'hover on the threshold'. As Chapter 3 discusses, accountability is a social construct, and its creation and application result from the interaction between the actor and the social structure. It can be studied only as a subjective creation that is situated within the social context and created by social actors. It is from this perspective, situating accountability within the highest tier of Williamson's framework, and recognising its relational characteristics, that Chapter 5 examines the operation of procedural accountability and the interaction between the two types of accountability as they exist in Tanzania.

This epistemology was applied in undertaking around 80 interviews (involving civil servants, politicians, donors, civil-society and non-governmental organisations, private-sector actors, the media and researchers), mainly in 2009 but also in 2010 and 2012.[1]

---

1   Civil servants, politicians and donors each comprised around one quarter of total interviewees, civil-society and non-governmental organisations represented 15 per cent. The remainder comprised the media, the private sector and researchers.

# Appendix 2

# A Model of Conditionality and Slippage

Each donor, D, desires policy reform, P; each recipient, R, desires financing, F. As each has to negotiate different combinations of financing and reform, their utility functions are $U=U(F,P)$. Therefore, $(UR_F>0)$ and $(UD_P>0)$. In Case 1, there are no restrictions; in Case 2, the recipient is resistant to policy reform. Conditionality, C, is represented as $P=CF$.

The optimal conditionality is along $P=CF$., where the utility of donors, UD, and that of recipients, UR, intersect at point e. If conditionality is too tight, represented as an anticlockwise pivot to $P=C_tF$, slippage will arise. Disbursement, even in the event of such slippage (and the resulting reduction in credibility), is tempting, as it would increase both UD and UR to e', as Figure A.1 shows.

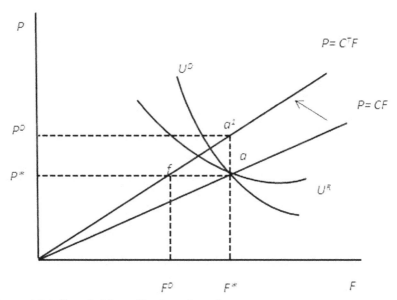

**Figure A2.1 Case 1: Mutually shared preferences**

*Source:* White and Morrissey 1997: 499

If, as in Case 2, there is conflict in the preference for reform, $(UR_P<0)$, with the budget constraint P*F*, the recipient's utility is maximised along URMAX at point c, and the donor's utility is maximised at point a. Therefore, the final outcome will be somewhere between a and c, and will be a function of bargaining between R and D, with the donor using tighter conditionality to move towards point a, through a rotation towards P=C$_T$F.

The recipient can play the game of agreeing to the tighter conditionality, knowing slippage will result. The slippage will move the outcome towards point d' in a single period game. However, in a repeated game, the credibility dilemma again emerges: whether to punish slippage in accordance with the conditionality agreement, or whether to disburse anyway and increase utility, as the donor can increase both UR and UD by disbursing anyway, moving up to point d.

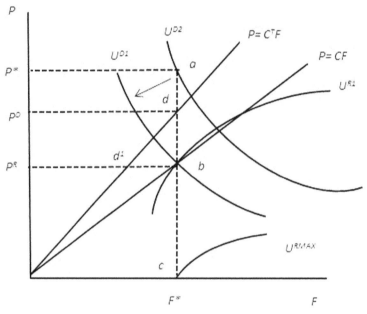

**Figure A2.2 Case 2: Conflict over preference for reform**

*Source*: White and Morrissey 1997: 501

# Bibliography

Acemoglu, D., and J. Robinson. 2007. *Persistence of power, elites and institutions.* Cambridge MA: Massachusetts Institute of Technology.

Acemoglu, D., Ticchi D., and Vindigni A. 2007. *Emergence and persistence of inefficient states.* Cambridge MA: Massachusetts Institute of Technology.

Adam, C.S., and S.A. O'Connell. 1999. Aid, taxation and development in sub-Saharan Africa. *Economics and Politics* 11: 225–253.

African Media Barometer. 2010. *The first home grown analysis of the media landscape in Africa: Tanzania 2010.* Windhoek: Friedrich-Ebert-Stiftung, the Media Institute of Southern Africa.

Ally, B. 2007. *More access to information in Tanzania? A follow-up study.* Edited by Rakesh Rajani. Dar es Salaam: HakiElimu.

Alvesson, M., C. Hardy, and B. Harley. 2004. *Reflecting on reflexive practices in organization and management theory.* Working Paper Series. Lund: Institute of Economic Research.

Ampiah, K., and S. Naidu. 2008. The Sino African relationship. in *Crouching tiger, hidden dragon: Africa and China.* Edited by K. Ampiah and S. Naidu. Scottsville: University of KwaZulu-Natal Press.

Andrews, M. 2010. *How far have public financial management reforms come in Africa.* CID Working Paper. Cambridge MA: Center for International Development at Harvard University.

Andrews, M. 2013. *The limits of institutional reform in development.* Cambridge: Cambridge University Press

Andrews, M., Pritchett, L. and Woolcock, M. 2012. *Escaping capability traps through problem-driven iterative adaptation.* Working Paper 299. Washington, DC: CGD.

Anon. 2007. *Orodha ya mafisadi (list of shame).* Dar es Salaam. Unpublished.

Bachrach, P., and M.S. Baratz. 1970. *Power and poverty: theory and practice.* New York: Oxford University Press.

Bana, B., and W. McCourt. 2006. Institutions and governance: public staff management in Tanzania. *Public Administration and Development* 26:395–403.

Baregu, M. 1994. The rise and fall of the one party state in Tanzania, *in Economic change and political liberalization in sub-Saharan Africa*, edited by Jennifer A. Widner. Baltimore, London: John Hopkins University Press.

Barkan, J.D. (ed.). 1994. *Beyond capitalism vs. socialism in Kenya and Tanzania.* London: Lynne Rienner Publishers.

Bates, R.H. 2001. *Prosperity and violence: the political economy of development.* New York: W.W. Norton and Company

— 2007. Political reform. *in the political economy of economic growth in Africa, 1960–2000*. Edited by B. Ndulu, S. O'Connell, R. Bates, P. Collier, and C. Soludo. Cambridge: Cambridge University Press.

Bates, R.H., and D.D. Lien. 1985. *A note on taxation, development and representative government.* Social Science Working Paper. Pasadena, California: California Institute of Technology.

Bayart, J-F. 1986. Civil society in Africa in *Political domination in Africa*, edited by P. Chabal. Cambridge: Cambridge University Press, 109–125.

BBC. 2008. Tanzanian PM to resign over graft. *BBC News 24*, 10 January 2008. Available at: http://news.bbc.co.uk/1/hi/world/africa/7232141.stm [accessed: 15/3/2012].

Beck, T., G. Clarke, A. Groff, P. Keefer, and P. Walsh. 2001. New tools in comparative political economy: the database of political institutions. *World Bank Economic Review* 15:165–176.

Berg-Schlosser, D., and R. Siegler. 1990. *Political stability and development: a comparative analysis of Kenya, Tanzania and Uganda*. London: Rienner.

Beynon, J. 2003. *Poverty efficient aid allocations – Collier/Dollar revisited.* ESAU Working Paper. London: ODI.

Bigsten, A. 2001. Tanzania, in *Aid and reform in Africa: lessons from ten case studies*, edited by S. Devarajan, D.R. Dollar, and T. Holmgren. Washington DC: World Bank.

Bird, R., J. Martinez-Vazquez, and B. Torgler. 2004. *Societal institutions and tax effort in developing countries*. International Studies Program Working Paper Series. Atlanta: International Studies Program, Andrew Young School of Policy Studies, Georgia State University.

Birdsall, N., A. Mahgoub, and W. Savedoff. 2010. *Cash on delivery: a new approach to foreign aid.* Washington DC: Center for Global Development.

Booth, D. 2005. The Africa Commission report: what about the politics? *Development Policy Review* 4: 493–498.

— 2010. *Towards a theory of local governance and public goods provision in sub-Saharan Africa*. Africa Power Politics Programme Working Paper. London: ODI.

— 2011. *Aid effectiveness: bringing country ownership (and politics) back in*. Africa Power Politics Programme Working Paper. London: ODI.

— 2012. *Development as a collective action problem: addressing the real challenges of African governance*. Synthesis report of the Africa Power and Politics Programme. London: ODI.

— 2013. *Facilitating development: an arm's length approach to aid.* Think piece. London: ODI.

Booth, D., A. Lawson, T. Williamson, S. Wangwe, and M. Msuya. 2004. *Joint evaluation of general budget support Tanzania 1995–2004: Phase 2 Report – preliminary assessment of efficiency and effectiveness of budget support and recommendations for improvements*. Dar es Salaam, London: Daima Associates Limited, ODI.

Bourdieu, P. 1977. *Outline of a theory of practice*. Cambridge: Cambridge University Press.

Bovens, M. 1998. *The quest for responsibility: accountability and citizenship in complex organisations*. Cambridge: Cambridge University Press.

Bratton, M., and C. Logan. 2006. *Voters but not yet citizens: the weak demand for vertical accountability in Africa's unclaimed democracies*. Afrobarometer Working Papers. Accra, Pretoria, Cotonou: Afrobarometer.

Bratton, M., and N. van de Walle. 1997. *Democratic experiments in Africa: regime transitions in comparative perspective*. Cambridge: Cambridge University Press.

Brautigam, D. 2002. Building leviathan: revenue, state capacity and governance. *IDS Bulletin* 33:10–20.

Brautigam, D., and S. Knack. 2004. Foreign aid, institutions and governance in sub-Saharan Africa. *Economic Development and Cultural Change* 52:255–286.

Buchanan, J.M. 1975. The samaritan's dilemma, in *Altruism, morality, and economic theory*, edited by E Phelps. New York: Russell Sage Foundation, 71–85.

Burnside, C., and D. Dollar. 1997. *Aid, policies and growth*. Washington DC: Macroeconomics and Growth Division, Policy Research Department, World Bank.

— 2004. *Aid, policies, and growth: revisiting the evidence*. World Bank Policy Research Working Paper 2834. Washington DC: World Bank.

Castellani, F. 2002. *A model of central bank's accountability*. HEI Working Papers. Geneva: Economics Section, The Graduate Institute of International Studies.

Castellani, F., and X. Debrun. 2005. *Central bank independence and the design of fiscal institutions*. IMF Working Paper. Washington DC: IMF.

CCM. 2010. *Ilani ya uchaguzi (election manifesto)*. Dodoma: CCM.

Chabal, P., and J-P. Daloz. 1999. *Africa works: disorder as a political instrument*. Oxford: James Currey.

Chandhoke, N. 2003. Governance and the pluralisation of the state: implications for democratic citizenship. *Economic and Political Weekly* 38(28): 2957–2968.

Chege, M. 1994. The return of multiparty politics, in *Beyond capitalism vs. socialism in Kenya and Tanzania*, edited by Joel D. Barkan. London: Lynne Rienner Publishers, 47–74.

Cheibub, J.A. 1998. Political regimes and the extractive capacity of governments: taxation in democracies and dictatorships. *World Politics* 50:349–376.

Claussen, J., and M.J. Assad. 2010. *Public expenditure tracking survey for primary and secondary education in mainland Tanza*nia. Dar es Salaam: United Republic of Tanzania.

Coate, S., and S. Morris. 1996. *Policy conditionality*. PIER working paper. Philadelphia: Penn Institute for Economic Research, University of Pennsylvania.

Cockerham, W.C., A. Thomas, and G. Lüschen. 1993. Max Weber, formal rationality, and health lifestyles. *The Sociological Quarterly* 34:413–428.

Collier, P. 1997. The failure of conditionality, in *Perspectives on aid and development*, edited by Catherine Gwin and Joan M. Nelson. Washington DC: Overseas Development Council.

— 1999. Learning from failure: the international financial institutions as agencies of restraint in Africa, in *The self-restraining state: power and accountability in new democracies*, edited by A. Schedler, L. Diamond, and M.F. Plattner. Boulder: Lynne Rienner Publishers, 313–330.

Cooksey, B. 2011. *Public goods, rents and business in Tanzania*. Background paper. London: Africa Power and Politics Programme, ODI.

Cooksey, B. 2012. *Politics, patronage and projects: the political economy of agricultural policy in Tanzania*, Working paper 040. Brighton: Political Economy of Agricultural Policy in Africa, Future Agricultures.

Cooksey, B., and T. Kelsall. 2011. *The political economy of the investment climate in Tanzania*. Research Report. London: Africa Power and Politics Programme, ODI.

Cornwall, A. 2007. Buzzwords and fuzzwords: deconstructing development discourse. *Development in Practice* 17:471–484.

Cornwall, A., and K. Brock. 2005. *Beyond buzzwords: poverty reduction, participation and empowerment in development policy*. Overarching Concerns Programme Paper. Geneva: United Nations Research Institute for Social Development.

Costello, M.J. 1996. Administration triumphs over politics: the transformation of the Tanzanian state. *African Studies Review* 39:123–148.

Coulson, A. (ed.). 1979. *African socialism in practice: the Tanzanian experience*. Nottingham: Spokesman.

Cox, R.W. 1979. Ideologies and the new international economic order: reflections on some recent literature. *International Organization* 33:267–302.

Dahl, R.A. 1957. The concept of power. *Behavioral Science* 2: 201–215.

— 1958. A critique of the ruling elite model. *The American Political Science Review* 52:463–469.

— 1968. A critique of the ruling elite model, in *C. Wright Mills and the power elite*, edited by G.W. Dornhoff and H.B. Ballard. Boston: Beacon Press, 25–36.

— 1989. *Democracy and its critics*. New Haven: Yale University Press.

Daunton, M. 2001. *Trusting leviathan: the politics of taxation in Britain 1799–1914*. Cambridge: Cambridge University Press.

De Haan, J., F. Amtenbrink, and S.C. Eijffinger. 1999. Accountability of central banks: aspects and quantification. *Banca Nazionale del Lavoro Quarterly Review*. 209: 169–193.

de Renzio, P., and W. Krafchik. 2007. *Lessons from the field: the impact of civil society budget analysis and advocacy in six countries*. Washington, DC: International Budget Project.

Development Partner Governance Working Group. 2008. *Accountability in Tanzania: an effort to quantify developments over recent years*. Dar es Salaam: Governance Working Group, Accountable Governance Cluster.

DFID. 2002. *International Development Act*. London: DFID.

DiMaggio, P., and W. Powell. 1991. Introduction, in *The new institutionalism in organisational analysis*, edited by W Powell and Paul DiMaggio. Chicago: University of Chicago Press, 1–40.

Dogan, M. 2003. Introduction: diversity of elite configurations and clusters of power. *Comparative Sociology* 2:1–15.

Douglas, M. 1986. *How institutions think*. London: Routledge.

Drori, G. 2008. Institutionalism and globalization studies, in *The Sage handbook of organizational institutionalism*, edited by R. Greenwood, C. Oliver, K. Sahlin, and R. Suddaby. London: Sage, 449–472

Dwivedi, O.P., and J.G. Jabbra. 1988. Public service responsibility and accountability, in *Public service accountability: A comparative perspective*, edited by J.G. Jabbra and O.P. Dwivedi. West Hartford: Kumarian Press.

Easterly, W. 2003. The cartel of good intentions: the problem of bureaucracy. *Foreign Aid Policy Reform* 5 (4): 223–250.

Ebrahim, A. 2009. Placing the normative logics of accountability in thick perspective. *American Behavioral Scientist* 52:885–904.

Eurodad. 2008. *Eurodad analysis of the outcome of Accra*. Brussels: Eurodad.

— 2008. *Harmonisation and alignment*. Brussels: The German Marshall Fund of the United States.

Evans, P.B., W.F. Lam, P. Heller, E. Ostrom, J. Fox, and M. Burawoy. 1996. Government action, social capital and development: creating synergy across the public-private divide. *World Development* 24:1119–132.

Ewald, J. 2011. *Challenges for the democratisation process in Tanzania. Moving towards consolidation 50 years after independence?* PhD thesis. Gothenburg: School of Global Studies.

Eyben, R. 2007. *Power, mutual accountability and responsibility in the practice of international aid: a relational approach*. Working Paper. Brighton: Institute of Development Studies.

— 2009. Hovering on the threshold: challenges and opportunities for critical and reflexive ethnographic research in support of international aid practice, in *Ethnographic practice and public aid*, edited by S. Hagberg and C. Widmark: Uppsala Studies in Cultural Anthropology.

Eyben, R., and S. Ladbury. 2006. *Building effective states: taking a citizens' perspective*. Citizenship in synthesis paper. Brighton: Development Research Centre, IDS.

FACEIT. 2009. *National governance and corruption survey: initial data workshop*. Dar es Salaam: The Prevention and Combating of Corruption Bureau.

Farhadian-Lorie, Z., and M. Katz. 1989. Fiscal dimensions of trade policy, in *Fiscal policy, stabilization, and growth in developing countries* edited by M.I. Blejer and K-Y. Chu. Washington DC: IMF, 276–306.

Fearon, J. 1999. Electoral accountability and the control of politicians: selecting good types versus sanctioning poor performance, in *Democracy, accountability and representation*, edited by A. Przeworski, S. Stokes, and B. Manin. Cambridge: Cambridge University Press, 55–97.

Fine, M., L. Weis, S. Weseen, and L. Wong. 2000. For whom? qualitative research, representations, and social responsibilities, in *Handbook of qualitative research*, edited by N.K. Denzin and Y.S. Lincoln. London: Sage Publications, 107–132.

Finnemore, M. 1996. Review: norms, culture, and world politics: insights from sociology's institutionalism. *International Organization* 50:325–347.

Fjeldstad, O.H. 2001. Taxation, coercion and donors: local government tax enforcement in Tanzania. *The Journal of Modern African Studies* 39: 289–306.

Fleck, L. 1979. *Genesis and development of a scientific fact*. Chicago: University of Chicago Press.

Foucault, M. 1979. *Discipline and punish*. Knopf Doubleday Publishing Group.

— 1998. *The History of sexuality: the will to knowledge*. London: Penguin.

Fox, J. 2007. The uncertain relationship between transparency and accountability. *Development in Practice* 17:663–671.

Freedom House. 2009. *Freedom in sub-Saharan Africa 2009: A survey of political rights and civil liberties*. Washington DC: Freedom House. Available at: http://www.freedomhouse.org/sites/default/files/Freedom%20in%20 Sub%20Saharan%20Africa.pdf [accessed: 12 March 2010].

— 2009. *Freedom of the press*. Washington DC: Freedom House. Available at: http://www.freedomhouse.org/report/freedom-press/freedom-press-2009 [accessed: 12 March 2010].

— 2009. *Tanzania country report*. Washington DC: Freedom House. Available at: http://www.freedomhouse.org/report/freedom-press/2009/tanzania [accessed: 12 March 2010].

— 2012. *Freedom in the world 2012: Tanzania*. Washington DC: Freedom House. Available at: http://www.freedomhouse.org/report/freedom-world/2012/ tanzania [accessed: 17 January 2013].

Funke, N., and H. Solomon. 2002. The shadow state in Africa: a discussion, in *Development Policy Management Forum Occasional Paper 5*. Addis Ababa: United Nations Economic Commission for Africa, 1–20.

Gaventa, J. 2003. *Power after Lukes: a review of the literature*. Brighton: Institute of Development Studies.

GBS donor group. 2008. *Challenges on combating corruption in Tanzania*. Dar es Salaam. Unpublished.

— 2008 Letter to Permanent Secretary MoFEA, Mr Khijjah. Unpublished.

GBS donor group and MoFEA. 2008. *Performance assessment framework draft* 5th December 2008. Dar es Salaam. Unpublished.

Geraats, P.M. 2002. Central bank transparency. *Economic Journal* 112:532–565.

Ghura, D. 1998. *Tax revenue in sub-Saharan Africa: effects of economic policies and corruption*. IMF Working Paper Washington, DC: International Monetary Fund.

Giddens, A. 1979. *Central problems in social theory: action, structure and contradiction in social analysis*. Berkeley, Los Angeles: University of California Press.

— 1984. *The constitution of society*. Cambridge: Polity Press.

Gill, S. 1990. *American hegemony and the trilateral commission*. Cambridge: Cambridge University Press.

Glennie, A., W. Straw, and L. Wild. 2012. *Understanding public attitudes to aid and development*. London: IPPR, ODI.

Gloppen, S., and L. Rakner. 2002. Accountability through tax reform? Reflections from sub-Saharan Africa. *IDS Bulletin* 33:30–40.

Goetz, A.M., and R. Jenkins. 2005. *Reinventing accountability: making democracy work for human development*. Basingstoke, Hampshire: Palgrave MacMillan.

Gore, C. 2000. The rise and fall of the Washington consensus as a paradigm for developing countries. *World Development* 28:789–804.

Gould, J. 2005. Timing, scale and style: capacity as governmentality in Tanzania, in *The aid effect: giving and governing in international development*, edited by D. Mosse and D. Lewis. London: Pluto Press.

Gould, J. (ed.). 2005. *The new conditionality*. London: Zed Books.

Governance Working Group. 2010. *Analysis of 2010 elections*. Dar es Salaam. Unpublished.

Gramsci, A. 1971. *Selections from the prison notebooks of Antonio Gramsci*. London: Lawrence and Wishart.

Grant, R.W., and R.O. Keohane. 2005. Accountability and abuses of power in world politics. *The American Political Science Review* 99:29–43.

Greenhill, R., Prizzon A., and Rogerson A. 2013. *The age of choice: developing countries in the new aid landscape*. ODI Working Paper 364. London: ODI

Grotius, H. 1625. *De jure belli ac pacis (on the law of war and peace)*. Indianapolis: Liberty Fund Inc. Available at: http://oll.libertyfund.org/index. php?option=com_staticxt&staticfile=show.php%3Fperson=3775&Itemid=28 [accessed: 10 February 2012].

Gulrajani, N. 2010. *Challenging global accountability: the intersection of contracts and culture in the World Bank*. GEG Working Paper 56. Oxford: University of Oxford.

Gupta, A. 1995. Blurred boundaries: the discourse of corruption, the culture of politics, and the imagined state. *American Ethnologist* 22:375–402.

Haan, A. de, and W. Warmerdam. 2012. *The politics of aid revisited: a review of evidence on state capacity and elite commitment*. ESID Working Paper Manchester. Manchester: Effective State and Inclusive Development Research Centre, University of Manchester.

Haggard, S. 1990. *Pathways from the periphery: the politics of growth in the newly industrialized countries*. New York: Cornell University Press.

Hansen, H., and F. Tarp. 2000. *Aid and growth regressions*. CREDIT Research Paper. Nottingham: Centre for Research in Economic Development and International Trade, University of Nottingham.

Harding, R., and L. Wantchekon. 2010. *The political economy of human development*. Human Development Research Paper. New York: UNDP.

Harrison, G. 2001. Post-conditionality politics and administrative reform: reflections on the cases of Uganda and Tanzania. *Development and Change* 32:657–679.

Harrison, G., and S. Mulley. 2007. *Tanzania: a genuine case of recipient leadership in the aid system?* Working Papers. Oxford: The Global Economic Governance Programme.

Hawksley, H. 2010. UK seeks China aid partnership in Africa. London: BBC. 5 October 2010. Available at: http://www.bbc.co.uk/news/world-africa-11444441 [accessed: 6 October 2010].

Helleiner, G. 2002. Local ownership and donor performance monitoring: new aid relationships in Tanzania? *Journal of Human Development* 3:251–261.

Helleiner, G., T. Killick, N. Lipumba, B. Ndulu, and K.E. Svendson. 2002. Development cooperation issues between Tanzania and its aid donors, in *NEPAD at Country Level – Changing Aid Relationships in Tanzania*, edited by S. Wangwe. Dar es Salaam: Mkuki na Nyota.

Hirschman, A. 1970. *Exit, voice and loyalty: responses to decline in firms, organisations and states*. Cambridge MA: Harvard University Press.

Hobbes, T. and Pogson, S. 1651, 1909. *Hobbes's Leviathan: reprinted from the edition of 1651 (1909)*. Oxford: Clarendon Press.

Hobson, J.M. 2001. The second state debate in international relations: theory turned upside-down. *Review of International Studies* 27:395–414.

Hu, Y. 2013. Chinese school rebuilt with African aid. In China Daily. Beijing. 28 March 2013. Available at: http://usa.chinadaily.com.cn/epaper/2013–03/28/content_16353221.htm [accessed: 28 March 2013].

Hyden, G. 1980. *Beyond ujamaa in Tanzania: underdevelopment and an uncaptured peasantry*. London: Heinemann Educational.

— 1994. Party, state and civil society: control versus openness, in *Beyond capitalism vs. socialism in Kenya and Tanzania*, edited by J.D. Barkan. London: Lynne Rienner Publishers.

— 2008. After the Paris declaration: taking on the issue of power. *Development Policy Review* 26:259–274.

— 2008. *Institutions, power and policy outcomes in Africa*. Discussion Paper. London: Africa Power and Politics Programme, ODI.

— 2010. *Political accountability in Africa: Is the glass half-full or half-empty?* Working Paper. London: Africa Power and Politics Programme, ODI.

Hyden, G., and M. Mmuya. 2008. Power and policy slippage in Tanzania – discussing national ownership of development. *Sida Studies 21*. Stockholm: Sida.

Hymer, S. 1979. *The multinational corporation: a radical approach*. Cambridge, England: Cambridge University Press.

Iliffe, J. 1971. *Agricultural change in modern Tanganyika: an outline history*. Nairobi East African Publishing House.

IMF. 2007. *The IMF and aid to sub-Saharan Africa*. Washington DC: IMF.

— 2009. Article IV consultation: Tanzania. *IMF country report*. Washington DC: IMF.

— 2013. Fifth review under the Policy Support Instrument: Tanzania. *IMF country report*. Washington DC: IMF.

International Budget Partnership. 2007. *Open budget questionnaire*. Washington, DC: International Budget Partnership.

Isaacman, A. 1996. *Cotton is the mother of poverty: peasants, work and rural struggle in colonial Mozambique, 1938–1961*. Portsmouth: Heinemann.

Jackson, R.H., and C.G. Rosberg. 1982. *Personal rule in black Africa: prince, autocrat, prophet, tyrant*. Berkeley: University of California Press.

Jelmin, K. 2012. *Democratic accountability in service delivery: a synthesis of case studies*. Stockholm: International Institute for Democracy and Electoral Assistance International IDEA.

Joseph, R. 1988. *Democracy and prebendal politics in Nigeria: the rise and fall of the second republic*. Cambridge: Cambridge University Press.

— 2012. *Beyond prebendalist systems: state, democracy and development in Africa*. Africa Plus.

Just Associates. 2007. *Making change happen 3: power. Concepts for revisioning power for justice, equality and peace*. Washington DC: Just Associates.

Kalberg, S. 1980. Max Weber's types of rationality: cornerstones for the analysis of rationalization processes in history. *The American Journal of Sociology* 85:1145–1179.

Kalebe-Nyamongo, C. 2009. *Self-interest vs. altruism: Malawian elites and poverty reduction*. DSA Annual Conference 2009: Contemporary Crises and New Opportunities. Ulster: 15 September 2009.

Kanbur, R. 2000. Aid, conditionality and debt in Africa. in *Foreign aid and development: lessons learnt and directions for the future*, edited by F. Tarp. London: Routledge.

Keefer, P. 2007. Clientelism, credibility, and the policy choices of young democracies. *American Journal of Political Science* 51:804–821.

Keefer, P., and S. Khemani. 2003. *Democracy, public expenditures and the poor*. Washington DC: Development Research Group, World Bank.

— 2005. Democracy, public expenditures, and the poor: understanding political incentives for providing public services. *World Bank Research Observer* 20:1–27.

Kelsall, T. 2002. Shop windows and smoke-filled rooms: governance and the re-politicisation of Tanzania. *Journal of Modern African Studies* 40:597–619.

— 2004. Contentious politics, local governance and the self. Goteborg: Nordiska Afrikainstitutet.

— 2008. *Going with the grain in African development?* Discussion Paper 1. London: Africa Power and Politics Programme, ODI.

Kelsall, T., D. Booth, D. Cammack, and F. Golooba-Mutebi. 2010. *Developmental patrimonialism? Questioning the orthodoxy on political governance and economic progress in Africa.* Working Paper 9. London: Africa Power and Politics Programme, ODI.

Kelsall, T., with D. Booth, D. Cammack, B. Cooksey, F. Golooba-Mutebi, Gebremichael M., and S. Vaughan. 2013. *Business, politics, and the state in Africa: challenging the orthodoxies on growth and transformation.* London: Zed Books.

Kelsall, T., S. Lange, S. Mesaki, and M. Mmuya. 2005. *Understanding patterns of accountability in Tanzania component 2: the bottom-up perspective.* London: Drivers of Change, DFID.

Kelsall, T., and M. Mmuya. 2005. *Accountability in Tanzania: historical, political, economic, sociological dimensions – a literature review for Drivers of Change.* Dar es Salaam: Drivers of Change, DFID.

Khan, M.H. 1996a. A typology of corrupt transactions in developing countries. *IDS Bulletin* 27 (2):12–21.

— 1996b. The efficiency implications of corruption. *Journal of International Development* 8 (5):683–696.

— 2004a. State failure in developing countries and institutional reform strategies, in *Towards pro-poor policies: aid, institutions, and globalization* edited by B. Tungodden, N. Stern, and I. Kolstad. Oxford, Washington DC: Oxford University Press and World Bank, 165–195. Available at: http://www-wds.worldbank.org/servlet/WDS_IBank_Servlet?pcont=details&e id=000160016_20040518162841 [accessed: 12 October 2009].

— 2004b. Corruption, governance and economic development, in *The new development economics,* edited by K.S. Jomo and B.Fine. New Delhi and London: Tulika Press and Zed Press.

Khan, M.H., and H. Gray. 2006. *State weakness in developing countries and strategies of institutional reform – operational implications for anti-corruption policy and a case study of Tanzania.* London: DFID. Unpublished.

Killick, T. 1995. *IMF programmes in developing countries.* London: Routledge.

— 1997. Principals, agents and the failings of conditionality. *Journal of International Development* 9:483–495.

Kiondo, A.S.Z. 1995. When the state withdraws, in *Liberalised development in Tanzania: studies on accumulation processes and local institutions*, edited by P. Gibbon. Uppsala: Nordiska Afrikainstitutet, 109–176.

Kiswahili Press Summary. 2010. Party resurrects Arusha Declaration, in *Rai.* Dar es Salaam: British High Commission. Unpublished.

Kjær, A.M., and O. Therkildsen. 2013. Competitive elections and agricultural sector initiatives in sub-Saharan Africa. In *Developing democracy: democratization, international stability and political renewal,* edited by M. Böss, J. Møller and S.-E. Skaaning. Copenhagen: Aarhus University Press. Forthcoming.

Kritzman, L., and M. Foucault. 1988, 1990. *Michel Foucault: politics, philosophy, culture – interviews and other writings 1977–1984.* London: Routledge.

Lachmann, R. 1990. Class formation without class struggle: an elite conflict theory of the transition to capitalism. *American Sociological Review* 55:398–414.

Lachmann, R. 2000. *Capitalists in spite of themselves: elite conflict and economic transitions in early modern Europe.* Oxford: Oxford University Press.

Leftwich, A. 2010. Beyond institutions. Rethinking the role of leaders, elites and coalitions in the institutional formation of developmental states and strategies. *Forum for Development Studies* 37:1–32. Paper read at Association of Development Researchers, 12 May 2009, at Copenhagen.

Leftwich, A., and C. Wheeler. 2011. *Politics, leadership and coalitions in development: findings, insights and guidance from the DLP's first Research and Policy Workshop.* A DLP Research and Policy Workshop Report. Frankfurt, 10 -11 March 2011. Available at: http://www.dlprog.org/ftp [accessed: 10 April 2012].

Leuthold, J.H. 1991. Tax shares in developing economies: a panel study. *Journal of Development Economics* 35:173–185.

Levi, M. 1988. *Of rule and revenue.* Berkeley: University of California Press.

Levy, B. 2010. Development trajectories: an evolutionary approach to integrating governance and growth. In *Economic Premise* 15. Washington DC: Poverty Reduction and Economic Management Network (PREM), World Bank.

Lijphart, A. 1969. Consociational democracy. *World Politics* 21:207–225.

Lipsky, M. 2010. *Street-level bureaucracy: dilemmas of the individual in public services.* New York: Russell Sage Foundation.

Lindemann, S., and J. Putzel. 2008. *State resilience in Tanzania.* London: London School of Economics.

Locke, J. 1689. *Second treatise of government.* Salt Lake City: Project Gutenberg EBook. 28 July 2010. Available at: http://www.gutenberg.org/files/7370/7370-h/7370-h.htm [accessed: 5 February 2011].

Lukes, S. 2005. *Power: a radical view.* London: Palgrave Macmillan.

MacDonald, P.K. 2003. Useful fiction or miracle maker: The competing epistemological foundations of rational choice theory. *The American Political Science Review* 97:551–565.

Mani, A., and S. Mukand. 2007. Democracy, visibility and public good provision. *Journal of Development Economics* 82:506–529.

Mann, M. 1993. *The sources of social power II: the rise of classes and nation-states, 1760–1914.* Cambridge: Cambridge University Press.

Mansbridge, J. 1998. *The many faces of representation.* Politics Research Group Working Paper. Cambridge, Massachusetts: John F. Kennedy School of Government.

Mattes, R. 2008. *The material and political bases of lived poverty in Africa: insights from the Afrobarometer.* Working Paper Series. Ann Arbor: Afrobarometer.

McCourt, W. 2012. Reconciling top-down and bottom-up: electoral competition and service delivery in Malaysia. *World Development* 40 (11):2329–2341.

Mcloughlin, C., and R.T. Batley. 2012. *The effects of sector characteristics on accountability relationships in service delivery.* ODI Working Paper 351. London: ODI.

Mearsheimer, J.J. 2001. *The tragedy of great power politics.* New York: Norton.

Médard, J-F. 1982. The underdeveloped state in tropical Africa: political clientelism or neo-patronialism, in *Private patronage and public power: political clientelism in the modern state*, edited by C. Clapham. London: Pinter, 162–92.

Mejía Acosta, A. with, A. Joshi, and G. Ramshaw. 2013. *democratic accountability and service delivery: a desk review.* Stockholm: International Institute for Democracy and Electoral Assistance.

Mercer, C. 1999. Reconceptualizing state-society relations in Tanzania: are NGOs making a difference? *Area* 31:247–258.

Meyer, J.W. 1987. The world polity and the authority of the nation-state, in *Institutional structure: constituting state, society and the individual*, edited by G. Thomas, J.W. Meyer, F. Ramirez, and J. Boli. London: Sage Publications, 41–70.

Meyer, J.W., J. Boli, and G. Thomas. 1987. Ontology and rationalization in the Western cultural account, in *Institutional structure: constituting state, society and the individual*, edited by G. Thomas, J.W. Meyer, F. Ramirez, and J. Boli. London: Sage Publications, 12–38.

Migdal, J.S. 1988. *Strong societies and weak states: state-society relations and state capabilities in the third world.* Chichester: Princeton University Press.

— 2001. *State in society: studying how states and societies transform and constitute one another.* Cambridge: Cambridge University Press.

Mill, J.S. 1861. *Representative government.* 25 February 2005. Available at: http://www.constitution.org/jsm/rep_gov.txt [accessed: 3 March 2010].

Mills, C.W. 1956, 2000. *The power elite.* New York: Oxford University Press.

Mmari, D., G. Sundet, H. Selbervik, and A. Shah. 2005. *Understanding patterns of accountability in Tanzania. Component 3: analysis of values, incentives and power relations in the budget process.* Oxford, Bergen and Dar es Salaam: Drivers of Change, DFID, Oxford Policy Management, Christian Michelsen Research Institute and REPOA.

Mmuya, M. 1998. *Political reform in eclipse: crises and cleavages in political parties.* Dar es Salaam: Friedrich Ebert Stiftung.

Molenaers, N., and R. Renard. 2011. *Policy dialogue: from discourse to practice.* Workshop in preparation of indicative co-operation programmes. Brussels, 9 February 2011.

Moore, M. 2001. Political underdevelopment: what causes bad governance. *Public Management Review* 3:385–418.

— 2004a. Revenues, state formation, and the quality of governance in developing countries. *International Political Science Review* 25:297–319.

— 2004b. Taxation and the political agenda: North and South. *Forum for Development Studies* 1:7–32.

— 2007. *How does taxation affect the quality of governance?* IDS Working Paper. Brighton: IDS.

— 2007. No representation without taxation. *Magazine for Development and Cooperation* 34(2):56–57. Available at: http://www3.giz.de/E+Z/content/archive-eng/02–2007/foc_art1.html [accessed: 4 November 2009].

Morrissey, O. 2004. Conditionality and aid effectiveness re-evaluated. *World Economy* 27:153–171.

Mosley, P., J. Harrigan, and J. Toye. 1995. *Aid and power: the World Bank and policy-based lending.* New York: Routledge.

Moss, T., and A. Subramanian. 2005. *After the big push? Fiscal and institutional implications of large aid increases.* CGD Working Paper. Washington, DC: Center for Global Development.

Muganda, A.A. 1997. *The war against corruption in Tanzania: overview of the report of the Presidential Commission on Corruption (Warioba Report)*, Delivered at the Integrity and Improvement Initiative and Developing Economies. Paris, 24–25 October 1997.

Murdoch, J., and T. Marsden. 1995. The spatialization of politics: local and national actor-spaces in environmental conflict. *Transactions of the Institute of British Geographers* 20:368–380.

Naschold, F., and A. Fozzard. 2002. *How, when and why does poverty get budget priority? Poverty reduction strategy and public expenditure in Tanzania.* London: Overseas Development Institute.

Newell, P., and J. Wheeler. 2006. *Rights, resources and the politics of accountability.* London: Zed Books.

Ngowi, H.P. 2005. *Institutional reforms to attract foreign direct investments (FDIs) as a strategy for economic growth: what has Tanzania done?* Globalization, Technology, and Sustainable Development Series. Brighton: Sussex University.

North, D. 2004. Economic performance through time. *American Economic Review* 84:359–368.

— 2005. *Understanding the process of economic change.* Woodstock: Princeton University Press.

North, D, J Wallis, S Webb, and B Weingast. 2007. *Limited access orders in the developing world.* Policy Research Working Paper. Washington DC: World Bank.

Nye, J.S. 2008. Public diplomacy and soft power. *The ANNALS of the American Academy of Political and Social Science* 616(1):94–109.

O'Neill, T., M. Foresti, and A. Hudson. 2007. *Evaluation of citizens' voice and accountability: review of the literature and donor approaches.* London: DFID.

O'Donnell, G. 1999. Horizontal accountability in new democracies, in *The self-restraining state: power and accountability in new democracies*, edited by A. Schedler, L. Diamond, and M.F. Plattner. London: Lynne Rienner Publishers, 29–51.

OECD. 2008a. *The Paris declaration on aid effectiveness and the Accra agenda for action.* Paris: OECD. Available at: http://www.ingentaconnect.com/content/oecd/16080254/2001/00002001/00000026/4301151e [accessed: 12 March 2010].

— 2008b. *The Accra high level forum (HLF3) and the Accra agenda for action*, Accra, 4th September, OECD. Available at: http://www.oecd.org/dac/ effectiveness/theaccrahighlevelforumhlf3andtheaccraagendaforaction.htm [accessed: 12 March 2010].

Okumu, J., and F. Holmquist. 1984. Party and party-state relations, in *Politics and public policy in Kenya and Tanzania*, edited by J.D. Barkan. New York, Eastbourne: Praeger.

Olowu, D. 2000. Bureaucracy and democratic reform, in *African perspectives on governance*, edited by G. Hyden, H.W.O. Okoth-Ogendo, and B. Olowu. Trenton, NJ: Africa World Press, 153–180.

Olson, M. 1965. *The logic of collective action*. Cambridge MA: Harvard University Press.

Ormrod, W., M. Bonney, and R. Bonney. 1999. *Crises, revolutions and self-sustained growth: essays in European fiscal history, 1130–1830*. Stamford: Stamford University Press.

Ortner, S.B. 1984. Theory in anthropology since the sixties. *Comparative studies in society and history* 26: 126–166.

Ostrom, E. 1990. *Governing the commons: the evolution of institutions for collective action*. Cambridge: Cambridge University Press.

— 1998. A Behavioral approach to the rational choice theory of collective action: presidential address, American Political Science Association, 1997. *The American Political Science Review* 92:1–22.

Oxfam. 1995. *The Oxfam poverty report*. Oxford: Oxfam.

Parsons, T., and E.A. Shils (eds). 1951, 1962. *Toward a general theory of action*. New York: Harper and Row.

Pastor, R. 1999. The third dimension of accountability: the international community in national elections, in *The self-restraining state: power and accountability in new democracies* edited by A. Schedler, L. Diamond, and M.F. Plattner. London: Lynne Rienner Publishers, 123–142.

Pinkney, R. 1997. *Democracy and dictatorship in Ghana and Tanzania*. New York: St. Martins Press.

Policy Forum. 2009. *Reforming allowances: a win-win approach to improved service delivery, higher salaries for civil servants and saving money*. Policy Brief. Dar es Salaam: Policy Forum with Twaweza.

— 2009. *Tanzania governance report 2006–07: Kikwete's first two years*. Dar es Salaam: Policy Forum.

— 2011. *Tanzania governance review 2010–11: economic growth without poverty reduction*. Dar es Salaam: Policy Forum.

Polsby, N.W. 1963. *Community power and political theory*. New Haven: Yale University Press.

Pritchett, L. 2002. *When will they ever learn? Why all governments produce schooling*. Cambridge MA: Kennedy School of Government. Available at http://www.hks.harvard.edu/fs/lpritch/education%20-%20docs/ed%20-%20 gov%20action/whenlearn_v1.pdf [accessed: 12 December 2012].

Public Financial Management Working Group.2009. *Public Financial Management Performance Report*. Dar es Salaam. Unpublished.

Rakner, Lise. 2005. *External accountability and PFM: Reflections from recent studies in Malawi, Uganda and Tanzania*. CAPE workshop on Aid, Budgets and Accountability. London, 3–4 October 2005. Available at: http://www. odi.org.uk/sites/odi.org.uk/files/odi-assets/events-presentations/594.pdf [accessed: 7 July 2009].

Rajani, R. (ed.) 2005. *Access to information in Tanzania: still a challenge*. Dar es Salaam: HakiElimu.

Rajani, R. 2007. *Accountability is political, not technical: citizens monitoring government in Tanzania*. Dar es Salaam: HakiElimu.

Ramirez, F., and J. Boli. 1987. Global patterns of educational institutionalization, in *Institutional structure: constituting state, society and the individual*, edited by G. M Thomas, J.W. Meyer, F Ramirez, and J. Boli. Newbury Park: Sage Publications, 150–172.

Reinharz, S. 1997. Who am I? The need for a variety of selves in fieldwork, in *Reflexivity and voice*, edited by R. Hertz. Thousand Oaks: Sage, 3–20.

Reis, E., and M. Moore. 2005. Elites, perceptions and poverties, in *Elite perceptions of poverty and inequality*, edited by E. Reis and M. Moore. London, New York: Zed Books, 1–25.

Reno, W. 2000. Clandestine economies, violence and states in Africa. *Journal of International Affairs* 53:433.

Richey, L. 1999. Family planning and the politics of population in Tanzania: international to local discourse. *The Journal of Modern African Studies* 37:457–487.

Robinson, W., and J. Harris. 2000. Towards a global ruling class? Globalization and the transnational capitalist class. *Science & Society* 64:11–54.

Robinson, W.I. 2010. *Global capitalism theory and the emergence of transnational elites*. Working Paper. Helsinki: UNU-WIDER.

Rocha Menocal, A., and B.J. Sharma. 2008. *Joint evaluation of citizens' voice and accountability: synthesis report*. London: DFID.

Rogerson, A. 2011. *What if development aid really rewarded results? Revisiting the cash-on-delivery (COD) aid model*. OECD Development Brief. Paris: OECD Development Co-operation Directorate.

Rousseau, J-J. 1762. *The social contract, or principles of political right*. The Constitution Society, 25 February 2005. Available at: http://www.constitution. org/jjr/socon.htm [accessed: 15 January 2013].

Routley, L. 2012. *Developmental states: a review of the literature*. ESID Working Paper. Manchester: Effective States and Inclusive Development Research Centre, University of Manchester.

Rweyemamu, D. 2009. *Strategies for growth and poverty reduction: has Tanzania's second PRSP influenced implementation?* DIIS/EPP Working Paper. Copenhagen: Danish Institute for International Studies.

Saiboko, A. 2012. *Tanzania: SUMA JKT reduces tractor prices*. 11 January 2012 Available at: http://allafrica.com/stories/201201120968.html [accessed: 23 March 2013].

Sawyerr, H. 1997. *Country-led aid coordination in Ghana*. Association for the Development of Education in Africa. Paris: Association for the Development of Education in Africa (ADEA). Available at: http://www.adeanet.org/ pubadea/publications/pdf/Country%20led%20ghana-eng.pdf [accessed: 17 September 2010].

Schedler, A. 1999. Conceptualizing accountability, in *The self-restraining state: power and accountability in new democracies* edited by A. Schedler, L. Diamond, and M.F. Plattner. London: Lynne Rienner Publishers, 13–28.

Schedler, A., L. Diamond, and M.F. Plattner. 1999. *The self-restraining state: power and accountability in new democracies*. London: Lynne Rienner Publishers.

Schmitter, P. 1999. Comments on O'Donnell: The limits of horizontal accountability, in *The self restraining state: power and politics in new democracies*, edited by A. Schedler, L. Diamond, and M.F. Plattner. London: Rienner Publishers Inc., 59–62.

Schumpeter, J.A. 1991 [1918]. The crisis of the tax state, in *The economics and sociology of capitalism*, edited by R.A. Swedberg. Princeton, NJ: Princeton University Press.

Sen, A. 1999. *Development as freedom*. Oxford: Oxford University Press.

Sewell, W.H., Jr. 1992. A theory of structure: duality, agency, and transformation. *The American Journal of Sociology* 98:1–29.

Shivji, I.G. 2006. *Let the people speak: Tanzania down the road to neo-liberalism*. Dakar: Codesria.

Simon, H.A. 1962. The architecture of complexity. *Proceedings of the American Philosophical Society* 106:467–482.

Simon, H.A. 1973. *Four essays on procedural rationality in economics*. Pittsburgh: Graduate School of Industrial Administration.

— 1985. Human nature in politics: the dialogue of psychology with political science. *American Political Science Review* 79:293–304.

Sitta, S., Slaa, W., Cheyo, J. and Ashurst, M. 2008. *Bunge lenye meno: a parliament with teeth for Tanzania*. London: Africa Research Institute.

Sklair, L. 2001. *The transnational capitalist class*. Oxford: Blackwell.

Sklar, R. 1986. Democracy in Africa, in *political domination in Africa*, edited by P. Chabal. Cambridge: Cambridge University Press, 17–29.

Skocpol, T. 1985. Bringing the state back in: strategies of analysis in current research, in *Bringing the state back in*, edited by P. Evans, D. Reuschmeyer, and T. Skocpol. New York: Cambridge University Press.

Sokomani, A. 2005. Money in Southern African politics. *African Security Review* 14:81–90.

Sussman, N. 2005. *Medieval public finances – the case of seingiorage in France*. Hebrew University 4 May 2005. Available at: http://economics.huji.

ac.il/facultye/sussman/Medieval%20public%20finances.pdf [accessed: 5 June 2009].

Svensson, J. 2000. When is foreign aid policy credible? Aid dependence and conditionality. *Journal of Development Economics* 61:61–84.

Tandon, Y. 2008. *Editorial: assessing Accra action agenda.* South Bulletin: Reflections and Foresights. Geneva: South Centre.

Tanzi, V. 1992. Structural factors and tax revenue in developing countries: a decade of evidence, in *Open economies: structural adjustment and agriculture*, edited by I. Goldin and A.L. Winters. New York: Cambridge University Press.

Tavakoli, H., R. Simson, and H. Tilley, with D. Booth. 2013. *Unblocking Results: using aid to address governance constraints in public service delivery.* London: ODI.

Taylor-Gooby, P., C. Hastie, and C. Bromley. 2003. Querulous citizens: welfare, knowledge and the limits to welfare reform. *Social Policy and Administration* 37:1–20.

Therkildsen, O. 2000. Public sector reform in a poor, aid-dependent country, Tanzania. *Public Administration and Development* 20:61–71.

— 2011. *Policy making and implementation in agriculture: Tanzania's push for irrigated rice.* DIIS/EPP Working Paper. Copenhagen: Danish Institute for International Studies.

Therkildsen, O. and F. Bourgouin. 2012. *Continuity and change in Tanzania's ruling coalition: legacies, crises and weak productive capacity.* DIIS/EPP Working Paper. Copenhagen: Danish Institute for International Studies.

ThisDay. 2008a. EPA fallout: Govt 'gambles' with 812bn/- donor money. Dar es Salaam: *ThisDay*, Media Solutions Ltd. 24 July 2008.

— 2008b. EPA scandal: donors still concerned by lack of prosecutions. Dar es Salaam: *ThisDay*, Media Solutions Ltd. 20 October 2008.

— 2008c. Revealed: The hidden costs of EPA scandal. Dar es Salaam: *ThisDay*, Media Solutions Ltd. 24 July 2008.

— 2008d. IMF gives thumbs up to EPA prosecutions: World Bank also happy, but warns. Dar es Salaam: *ThisDay*, Media Solutions Ltd. 24 December 2008.

— 2009a. *CCM to split?* Dar es Salaam: ThisDay, Media Solutions Ltd. 11 November 2009.

— 2009b. Tanzania loses ground in global anti corruption drive. Dar es Salaam: *ThisDay* Media Solutions Ltd. 18 November 2009.

Thompson, E. 1978. *The poverty of theory and other essays.* London: Merlin Press.

Thornton, N., and H.E. Meena. 2010. *Political economy and drivers of change analysis of climate change in Tanzania.* Dar es Salaam: DFID.

Tilley, H. 2013. *Unblocking Results: rural water in Tanzania.* London: ODI.

Tilly, C. 1992. *Coercion, capital and European states, AD 990–1992.* Oxford: Blackwell.

Tripp, A.M. 2012. *Donor assistance and political reform in Tanzania.* UNU-Wider Working Paper. Helsinki: UNU Wider.

Ullrich, K. 2003. *Independence and accountability of a central bank in a monetary union*. Mannheim, Germany: Centre for European Economic Research.

UNDP. 2007. *Project document: deepening democracy in Tanzania*. Dar es Salaam: UNDP.

— 2010. *Human development research paper*. New York: UNDP.

— 2012. *China strengthened partnership*. New York: UNDP. Unpublished.

United Republic of Tanzania. 2001. *Memorandum of understanding on performance assessment framework: poverty reduction budget support monitoring framework 2001–2004*. Dar es Salaam: Ministry of Finance. Unpublished.

— 2008a. *General budget support annual review 2008 final report*, edited by Ministry of Finance and Economic Affairs. Dodoma: Ministry of Finance and Economic Affairs.

— 2008b. *Reports of the Controller and Auditor General for the financial year ended 30th June 2007*, edited by National Audit Office. Dar es Salaam: Ministry of Finance.

— 2010. 2009. *Public financial management performance report*. Dar es Salaam: Public Financial Management Working Group. Unpublished.

— 2012a. *Views of the people*, edited by MKUKUTA Monitoring System. Dar es Salaam: Ministry of Planning, Economy and Empowerment and Research and Analysis Working Group. Final draft. December.

— 2012b. *A summary report of procurement audits in one hundred and twenty one procuring entities: FY2011/12*. Dar es Salaam: Public Procurement Regulatory Authority. Available at: http://www.ppra.go.tz/portal/index.php?view=library_doc&opt=opt&type=6&search=q [accessed: 14 January 2013].

— 2013. *Aid management platform: analysis of ODA portfolio for FY 2010/11 and 2011/12*, edited by External Finance Department Ministry of Finance and Economic Affairs. Dar es Salaam: Ministry of Finance and Economic Affairs. Available at: http://www.mof.go.tz/mofdocs/msemaji/AMP%20ODA%20ANNUAL%20REPORT.pdf [accessed: 20 April 2013].

Unsworth, S. 2010. *An upside down view of governance*. Brighton: IDS.

Urban, F., Mohan G., and Y. Zhang. 2011a. *The understanding and practice of development in China and the European Union*. IDS Working Paper. Brighton: IDS.

Urban, F., J. Nordensvärd, Y. Wang, D. Khatri, and Mohan G. 2011b. *China and the African oil sector: channels of engagement, motives, actors and impacts*. IDS Working Paper. Brighton: IDS.

Van de Walle, N. 2007. Meet the new boss, same as the old boss?, in *Patrons, clients and policies: patterns of democratic accountability and political competition*, edited by H. Kitschelt and S. Wilkinson. Cambridge: Cambridge University Press, 50–67.

Van der Pijl, K. 1984. *The making of an Atlantic ruling class*. London: Verso.

— 1989. The international level, in *The capitalist class: an international study*, edited by T. Bottomore and R.J. Brym. New York: New York University Press.

— 1998. *Transnational classes and international relations*. London: Routledge.

Water and Sanitation Program. 2011. *The political economy of sanitation: how can we increase investment and improve service for the poor? Operational experiences from case studies in Brazil, India, Indonesia, and Senegal.* Washington DC: Water and Sanitation Program, World Bank. Available at: http://www.wsp.org/sites/wsp.org/files/publications/WSP-Political-Economy-of-Sanitation.pdf [accessed: 4 October 2012].

Weber, M. 1919, 1991. Politics as vocation, in *From Max Weber: essays in sociology*, edited by H.H. Gerth, B.S. Turner, and C.W. Mills. Abingdon: Routledge.

Weghorst, K., and S. Lindberg. 2010. *Effective opposition strategies: a foundation for improved quality of government.* Gothenburg: University of Gothenburg.

Weisband, E., and A. Ebrahim. 2007. Introduction: forging global accountabilities, in *Global accountabilities: participation, pluralism, and public ethics*, edited by A. Ebrahim and E. Weisband. Cambridge: Cambridge University Press, 1–24.

White, H., and O. Morrissey. 1997. Conditionality when donor and recipient preferences vary. *Journal of International Development* 9:497–505.

Wild, L., V. Chambers, M. King, and D. Harris. 2012. *Common constraints and incentive problems in service delivery.* Working Paper. London: ODI.

Williamson, O.E. 2000. The new institutional economics: taking stock, looking ahead. *Journal of Economic Literature* 38:595–613.

World Bank. 2003. *Making services work for the poor.* The world development report 2004. Washington DC: World Bank.

— 2004. *Public expenditure management country assessment and action plan (AAP): Tanzania.* Washington DC: World Bank.

— 2005. *Program document for a proposed credit to United Republic of Tanzania for poverty reduction support credit 3.* Washington, DC: World Bank.

— 2008. *Program document for a proposed credit to United Republic of Tanzania for a sixth poverty reduction support credit.* Washington, DC: World Bank.

— 2009. *Ethiopia public finance review.* Washington DC: Poverty Reduction and Economic Management Africa Region, World Bank.

— 2012. *Implementation completion and results report to the United Republic of Tanzania for an accountability, transparency and integrity project.* Washington, DC: World Bank.

World Bank, and IMF. 2005. *Review of PRSPs.* Washington DC: World Bank, IMF.

Xiaoqing, Y., and Calkins J. 2013. *Tanzania Ambassador on Sino-Tanzania ties.* Beijing: China.org.cn. March 21 2013. Available at: http://www.china.org.cn/video/2013–03/21/content_28315641.htm [accessed: 24 March 2013].

# Index

9 781138 247185